COMPACT
CYMRU

CW00794230

# Welsh Pirates and Privateers

## Terry Breverton

Gwasg Carreg Gwalch

First published in 2018
© text: Terry Breverton
© publication: Gwasg Carreg Gwalch 2018

ISBN: 978-1-84524-281-7
Cover design: Eleri Owen

Published by Gwasg Carreg Gwalch,
12 Iard yr Orsaf, Llanrwst, Wales LL26 0EH
tel: 01492 642031
email: books@carreg-gwalch.cymru
website: www.carreg-gwalch.cymru

## About the Author

Terry Breverton is a Fellow of the Chartered
Institute of Marketing, and a Fellow of the
Institute of Consultancy. He studied in the
universities of Manchester and Lancaster, has
had a career in international management
consultancy, and has been a board level
director of multinational companies. He has
written over 50 books, mainly upon Welsh
history, heritage and culture, and has been
awarded the Welsh Books Council's 'Book of
the Month' upon five occasions. His books have
been translated into over 20 languages,
including Polish, Turkish, Japanese and
Chinese.

# Contents

# Introduction

In Wales, we tend to remember in literature our ministers and politicians, and their often empty lives, and ignore far more worthy men and women. Thus hardly anyone knows the story of the entrapment and murder of Llywelyn ap Gruffudd in 1282, and that Edward I then personally invented and supervised the prolonged hanging, drawing and quartering of his brother Prince Dafydd in 1283. Before this time, those gulty of 'treason' were already dead by hanging, before being slowly and ritually castrated and disembowelled. Edward I, written of as a hero, was in reality an illiterate butcher. As a youth he had cut off the ear and gouged out the eye of a young nobleman, who had not bowed low enough to him. After the defeat of Simon de Montfort (the father of Llywelyn's wife) at Evesham, Edward had him killed, and his head and genitalia were cut off and sent to Lady Matilda, the wife of Lord Roger Mortimer at Wigmore. Edward's campaigns across Wales employing foreign mercenaries were paid for by fines and dispossession of Jews, and loans from the greatest Italian banker. He reneged on the loans, causing the banker to fail, then loaned monies from an Italian bank again to build his 'Iron Ring' of castles, and again failed to repay, with the same results. The English conquest was only achieved by fraud enabling overwhelming resources to be directed against Cymru. Edward I, *'The Hammer of the Scots'* failed to conquer Scotland because his finances were drained in Welsh campaigns and no banker would finance him any longer. This is not taught in history books (see this author's *100 Greatest Welshmen* for more information upon Welsh heroes).

The 'dangerous' line of the Princes of Gwynedd was swiftly eradicated except for 'Yvain de Galles', a hero across the Continent, until an assassin was sent to Mortagne-sur-Mer in kill Owain Lawgoch in 1378. In 1401 Llywelyn ap Gruffydd Fychan refused to betray Owain Glyndŵr, and was slowly disembowelled before the usurper Henry IV. Llywelyn's refusal allowed the Glyndŵr War of Independence to carry on for another fourteen years, surviving multiple invasions from far greater forces. Welsh, i.e. British, history has hardly been taught in schools, but from the age of over a

## A GENERAL HISTORY OF THE

*Robberies and Murders*

Of the most notorious

## PYRATES,

AND ALSO

Their *Policies, Discipline* and *Government,*

From their firft RISE and SETTLEMENT in the Ifland
of *Providence,* in 1717, to the prefent Year 1724.

WITH

The remarkable ACTIONS and ADVENTURES of the two Female Pyrates, *Mary Read* and *Anne Bonny.*

To which is prefix'd

An ACCOUNT of the famous Captain *Avery* and his Com
panions; with the Manner of his Death in *England.*

The Whole digefted into the following CHAPTERS;

Chap. I. Of Captain *Avery.*
II. The Rife of Pyrates.
III. Of Captain *Martel.*
IV. Of Captain *Bonnet.*
V. Of Captain *Thatch.*
VI. Of Captain *Vane.*
VII. Of Captain *Rackam.*

VIII. Of Captain *England.*
IX. Of Captain *Davis.*
X. Of Captain *Roberts.*
XI. Of Captain *Worley.*
XII. Of Captain *Lowther.*
XIII. Of Captain *Low.*
XIV. Of Captain *Evans.*

And their feveral Crews.

To which is added,

A fhort ABSTRACT of the Statute and Civil Law, in.
Relation to PYRACY.

By Captain CHARLES JOHNSON.

LONDON, Printed for *Ch. Rivington* at the *Bible* and *Crown* in St.
*Paul's Church-Yard, J. Lacy* at the *Ship* near the *Temple-Gate,* and
*J. Stone* next the *Crown* Coffee-houfe the back of *Greys-Inn,* 1724.

*Frontispiece of the 1724 'A General History ... Pyrates' – with Davis, Roberts and John Evans receiving a chapter each*

*Black Bart Roberts*

thousand saints when England and Ireland were pagan, its history has been one of fifteen hundred years of invasion, during which all the cathedral scriptoria were destroyed, libraries burnt and churches sacked. Much of Welsh history has been deliberately destroyed, with the result that Anglophiles like Neil Kinnock can confidently state that Wales has no history worth knowing about.

This author has always written from a Welsh perspective, whether upon saints or sinners, including several books upon pirates and privateers. Most people have heard of Blackbeard and Captain Kidd, but they were very minor characters during the '*Golden Age of Piracy*', which ended with the death of John Roberts (Bart Roberts) of Casnewydd Bach. Wales can boast, if that is the correct term, of Black Bart Roberts, '*the most famous pirate in history*'; Henry Morgan, the most successful privateer in history; Hywel (Howell) Davis, '*the Cavalier Prince of Pirates*'; and John Callice, '*the most dangerous Pyrate in the realm*'. Another Welsh privateer, William Williams, was captured by the Spanish, marooned, wrote America's first novel (*The Journal of Llewellin Penrose – Seaman*), and taught America's most famous artist, Benjamin West, to paint! Many other Welsh pirates and privateers have had to be omitted for lack of space, but can be found in my *The Book of Welsh Pirates and Buccaneers*. In Stevenson's *Treasure Island*, he writes of Roberts' leading men hanging in chains, but we only see five real pirates. Apart from the Westcountrymen Edward England and Israel Hands (who sailed under Roberts), they were Roberts, Robert's Welsh surgeon Peter Scudamore and Davis.

Why did so many seamen become pirates? Seamen, whether from the Royal Navy or merchant fleets, were mainly forcibly pressed men, not volunteers, who were treated abominably, and not allowed to go on to dry land for fear of desertion. The crew on slavers had an average life expectancy of eighteen months at sea. The ships were under-manned, so men were overworked, and also fed disgusting rations in disease-ridden conditions. There were not many old 'sea-dogs'. The opportunity to join what pirates called their 'Commonwealth,' (literally a wealth-sharing community) where there were neither masters nor beatings, was a welcome one. Everyone had equal shares, and the captain was only 'captain' in times of battle or chase. When Roberts decided to succeed Howell Davis as a pirate captain, he gave us the origin of the saying '*a short life and a merry one*'.

## WILLIAM MARSH, de MARISCO (of the marshes), SIR WILLIAM DE MARISH fl. 1235-1242

Prince Madog ab Owain Gwynedd was said to have sailed from Lundy Island (among other possible locations) to discover America around 1170, and it was used as a pirate sanctuary until the 1300's. William Marsh, son of a justicier in Ireland, married the niece of the Archbishop of Dublin, and received a rich dowry. He was expected to have a long and successful career at court in London, but had an ungovernable temper. Marsh murdered a king's messenger, Henry Clement, at the gates of Henry III's Westminster Palace in 1235. He was outlawed, and fled to Lundy, nominally a possession of his cousin, and until 1242 used it as his base to prey on Western shipping. According to Matthew Paris, 'William Marsh, son of Geoffrey Marsh, took up his quarters on an island near Bristol, called Lundy, a place impregnable by the nature of its situation, where he lived like a pirate with a number of proscribed and wicked men, indulging in plunder and rapine, and, attended by his companions, traversed the places on the neighbouring coast, despoiling the inhabitants of their property, especially wine and other provisions. By sudden incursions lie frequently carried off vast booty from the country lying near the island, and in many ways injured the kingdom of England both by land and sea, and caused great loss to the native and foreign merchants.' Marsh also used Sully Island, between Barry and Penarth, as a base.

Marsh seized shipping from the Mull of Galloway down to Land's End, and became a friend of the King of Scotland for damaging English commerce and trade. Marsh also traded with the monks of Margam Abbey*, where he sometimes stayed. His main income came from ransoming his captives, kept in a dismal damp dungeon in Lundy's castle keep, rather than disposing of cargoes.

In 1542, Marsh was arraigned for High Treason, as he had sent a servant to assassinate Henry III at his palace at Woodstock. This may have been at the instigation of the Scottish king. The coast of Devon was specially defended against Marsh's attacks, and some of his men and his wife were captured. Sea-going nobles

*Lundy Island and its famous Marisco Tavern*

Welsh Pirates and Privateers    9

advised the king that Marsh was safe upon his impregnable Lundy stronghold, and that only treachery could undo him. Thus Marsh was betrayed when one of his captured men, forced by the thumbscrew, told the royal forces that the weak point in his defences

*William de Marisco being dragged to his execution*

was held by a single guard, who did not like Marsh. Marsh was in the process of building a large new galley, but was captured in May 1242 while eating his dinner, slung into Bristol Castle prison and then and taken in irons to the Tower of London. He and 16 colleagues were dragged by horses to the gallows and hung, with Marsh being hung, drawn and quartered, the penalty for treason. Other members of his crew were executed at Newgate. The new ship that he had been constructing at Lundy was taken to Ilfracombe to be finished and put into the Crown's service. (The *Marisco Tavern* is Lundy's pub – the island is now owned by the Landmark Trust, and a marvellous place for a holiday.)

Mathew Paris recorded '*On the feast of St. James, by the king's order, the said William, with sixteen of his accomplices taken with him, was tried and condemned, and, by the king's order, was sentenced to an ignominious death. He was, therefore, first dragged from Westminster to the Tower of London, and from thence to that instrument of punishment called a gibbet [gallows] suspended on which he breathed forth his miserable life. After he had grown stiff in death, his body was let down and disembowelled; his entrails were immediately burnt on the spot, and his wretched body divided into four parts, which were sent to the four principal cities of the kingdom, that the sight of them might strike terror into all beholders. His sixteen accomplices were all dragged through London at the horse's tail, and hung on gibbets. The said William, after his condemnation, when about to udergo the sentence pronounced upon him, invoking the divine judgment to witness, boldly declared that he was entirely free and guiltless of the crime of treason imputed to him, and likewise of the murder of the aforesaid clerk Clement; he also asserted that he had betaken himself to the aforesaid island for no other reason than to avoid the king's anger, which he had always above all things wished to pacify by submitting to any kind of trial, or by any other humiliation; but that, after he had taken refuge as a fugitive in the said island, he was obliged to prolong his miserable life by seizing on provisions wherever he could find them. He then poured out his soul in confession before God, to J. de St. Giles, one of the brethren of the Preacher order, and confessed his sins with contrition, not excusing himself and giving vent to evil words, but rather accusing himself. This discreet preacher and confessor then administered gentle comfort to him, and dismissed him in peace, persuading him that he underwent the death to which he was doomed by way of repentance. And thus, as before mentioned, horrible to relate, he endured not one, but several dreadful deaths.'*

*In 1289, the Prior of Goldcliffe Abbey in Gwent, was accused by a Bristol merchant of receiving several tuns of Bordeaux wine from his wrecked ship. The Vicars of Portishead and Ash in Somerset also shared in the booty. Monasteries were like local gentry, benefiting from smuggling and piracy.

## WALTER HERBERT fl. 1537

Captain Richard Hose's London ship, *Valentine*, put into Cogan (Penarth) in 1537, carrying wine, salt, tunny fish and alum. Hose was accused of failing to pay harbour dues, and put into prison. He was also carrying some Portuguese refugees, which did not help his case. Walter Herbert, Cardiff's Custom officer, illegally sailed the ship to Chepstow and sold the Valentine and its cargo. His defence was that he had been instructed to do so by his Herbert kinsman, Henry Somerset, Earl of Worcester, whose mother was Baroness

Elizabeth Herbert. Thomas Cromwell released Walter in 1538, with no charges being proven for this act of piracy. The Herbert family controlled south-east Wales at this time and for decades after. The Piracy Commissioners in 1565 included William Herbert of St Julian (Newport), William Herbert of Coldbrook, William Herbert of Swansea, Edward Mansel and Thomas Lewis of the Van (Caerphilly), all of whom were closely connected to William Herbert, Earl of Pembroke, and all of whom were involved in incidents of piracy and receiving.

## JOHN PHILLIPS (PHELYPPES)
### fl. 1540 – *'the first captain known to have committed piracy in the Americas'*

In March 1540, Phillips left Portsmouth in the *Barbara*, sailing for Brazil, with around 100 crewmen. His crew included a dozen French sailors, who had been involved in raids in the Americas. Phillips had the distinction of being the first British seaman to have practised piracy in the New World. Off Portugal's Cape St Vincent, Phillips took a 40-ton French barque carrying salt, and then a Spanish caravel with gold and amber from the Barbary Coast. He took the captured barque as his new *Barbara*, before putting into the Canary Islands for water and provisions for the Atlantic Crossing. The barque, or bark, had three masts, the first two being square-rigged and the after mast fore and aft rigged. Highly manoeverable and with a shallow draft, the vessel became the favoured pirate ship in the Caribbean, and they also sailed across to Africa and Madagascar, carrying up to 90 men.

In May, Phillips made landfall near Pernambuco (modern Recife, in Brazil), but found no ships to ransack, nor anything worth stealing from the natives. He headed northwest, for *'The Land of the Cannibals'*. Eight men disappeared on shore, and he sailed on to Hispaniola (now Haiti and the Dominican Republic). Off Santo Domingo, Phillips took a 300-ton Spanish vessel loaded with cow-hides and sugar. However, a Spanish galleon caused some damage to the *Barbara*, and Phillips escaped to Western Hispaniola. He transferred loot off the damaged *Barbara* to the captured Spanish ship. He Spanish crew was set ashore, and Phillips shared out gold between his men. After a stormy crossing back, reaching England in November, there were formal Spanish complaints, and several of the 32 surviving crewmen were arrested. However, it seems that no-one was tried. The insurers paid the *Barbara's* owners for her loss, although she had been lost committing piracy.

## CAPTAIN OWEN fl. 1540

In 1540, he was the captain of a pirate barque operating from Mount's Bay, and murdered a Breton crew off the Scillies. One of his crew recounted: '*Captain Owen called to Phillip the Welshman and to the other Welshman, speaking in Welsh, and at one or two of the clock in the afternoon the said Phillip called up the Bretons one after another to the number of seven men and brought every man to the waist of the ship and caused John the mariner of Weymouth to bind their hands on cross behind their backs. Then the same John by command of Phillip cast the seven Bretons overboard in the sea ... They were drowned with their jerkin on them, about 4 leagues from the land.*' Just two hours later, Captain Owen ordered the crew of another Breton hoy (a small coastal vessel) to be thrown into the sea.

## WALTER VAUGHAN fl. 1542

Dunraven had the worst reputation for wrecking on the Glamorgan coast – its great castle-mansion was unfortunately demolished in 1962, but it is an ancient site with an Iron Age fort overlooking the beautiful sandy beach of Southerndown. Spencer's *Annals of South Glamorgan* tell us of Walter Vaughan, the 16th century Lord of Dunraven, who took to wrecking to supplement the income from his estates. From Bredwardine, he owned the estate from marrying Ann, the last of the Butler family in 1541. To supplement his wasteful extravagances, he took to wrecking. His main accomplice was '*Matt of the Iron Hand*', a villain who had lost his hand in a previous fight at sea with Vaughan's men. Vaughan did not know that this hook-handed lieutenant secretly hated him, and wished for revenge. One of the techniques used to lure ships onto the rocks was to fix lanterns to cattle. Ships in trouble would head towards the 'harbour' and get dragged onto a lee shore.

On a dark and stormy night, after several years of luring ships to their fate with false lights, Matt eventually wrecked the boat he wanted more than any other.

He reported his success to Walter Vaughan, who queried if there were any survivors. '*There was just the one, a Welshman from Dunraven*', Matt laughed back at him, as he thrust a severed hand into Vaughan's face. On the fingers was the ring of Vaughan's only son. Tradition states that Matt was then shot dead by the family harper, and Vaughan was so heart-broken that he sold the castle and left the area, never to return.

### SIR JOHN WOGAN fl. 1542-1555

In the 1530's, Tenby had become a favourite haunt of Breton pirates. Around

*Dunraven*      *(opp) Tenby and Ilfracombe*

fifteen, including Captain John du Laerquerec, were taken when they came ashore to reprovision. Three boats were sent from the pirate ship to rescue their captain: '*iii bootes came to the said tonne about midnight intending to have snatched the captain from them by force, but when they could not so have him, they shot their gonnes and blew up their trumpets and departed.*' Upon examination, the captain admitted '*he had taken from Englishmen, ropes of ships, mariners' apparel, v pieces of wine, fish, one crown of gold and xv half pens or pens of*

silver, iiiv daggers and a converture called in French "une port de ray"...' His defence of his actions were that other St Malo pirates were much worse than him, such as '*John Hacque, who hath pilled and robbed many Englishmen*'.

In 1542 Tenby features again, when Sir John Wogan, a former Sheriff of Pembroke, was suspected of complicity in gold stolen from a French ship. (Nearly all the Welsh gentry seemed to be complicit in smuggling and lawlessness, from this time through to the mid-nineteenth century). Later, in 1555 some pirates took a Breton merchant ship and took it to Tenby, to be arrested by Wogan. His next move was to sell the cargo and pocket the proceeds. John le Barthicke, the owner, petitioned the Privy Council, who ordered Wogan to return the money. In 1556, Welsh merchants petitioned about the pirate Mericke Morgan, and with piracy in the Bristol Channel and Irish Sea being worse than anywhere else in Britain, Elizabeth I issued orders that all convicted pirates should be executed '*upon some cliffs near to the sea-side*', their captains to be hanged in chains in view of the shipping lanes to discourage the others.

## MICHAEL JAMES fl. 1546

Sailing the *Mary Figge* of Plymouth, he pillaged Flemish ships, and forced a Spanish ship sailing to Chester, to surrender in 1546. James put the crew under the hatches for two days and nights while he looted the cargo. He then imprisoned them in the bread-house before abandoning the ship, '*where they had no space to stand nor sit but did lie upon one another like hogs, fast bound with ropes and cords.*' James later claimed that he did this because the Spanish had tortured his father. He had threatened to sink the ship with its crew tied up, but he later freed the Spaniards, and sold the cargo in Cardiff and Bristol. Several pirates named James are mentioned in piracy cases in 1546, along with James Hughes at Brighton and William ap Howell at Rye.

## RICHARD VAUGHAN fl. 1546

Sailing out of Calais, he was reported as the ringleader of pirates in 1546 by the Mayor of Haverfordwest, having captured a Portuguese caravel, the *Sancta Maria de Leusa*, off the Pembroke coast, and disposing of the booty in Pembrokeshire and possibly also in Ilfracombe.

## MORGAN MATTHEW fl. 1548

Probably from the famous Matthew family of Radyr, St Ffagan's and Llandaff, on Easter Day 1548 Morgan Matthew commanded the *Mathewe de Kerdiff* and the *Valentine* of Topsham, taking a Breton ship off the north coast of Spain. The ship was sailing from Spain. The pirates *'fell in with spoiling and braking open of chests and within the space of half an hour they had rifled the said Breton; and the company departed with their spoil, being conveyed in bread-sacks.'* Matthew's nineteen pirates found their capture was carrying the servants and baggage of the Portuguese Ambassador to France, Brasdellus Vetto. They looted six tables and silverware intended for the embassy – 880 ounces of silver flasks, flagons, porringers, platters, bowls and basins worth £220 at the time. Four cases of 'wild-fire' (incendiary grenades) for defending the ship were also stolen. The pirates kept their gains, although they were prosecuted, and were given a free pardon in 1551.

## GRIFFITHS OF CEFNAMWLCH fl. 1563

Anglesey and Caernarfonshire and their associated islands were the most popular pirate haunts in North Wales, usually supported by local gentry such as the Bulkeleys of Anglesey and the Griffiths family of Cefnamwlch on the Llŷn peninsula. In 1563 Captain Thomas Wolfall captured a prize with a cargo of wheat and rye, which he took to Ynys Enlli (Bardsey isle). Griffiths boarded the prize to confiscate it, but Wolfall claimed that he was carrying a letter of marque issued by the Earl of Warwick. Griffiths appealed to Vice-Admiral Sir Richard Bulkeley, Sheriff William Griffiths and Griffith Davies, the keeper of the Armoury, for support, but they refused.

Griffiths then plotted with John Thane to pretend to buy corn from Wolfall, and then attacked the pirate ship with sixty men, in return for a payment to Thane of £30. Griffiths' plot was betrayed and corn and wheat were sold openly at Barmouth. John Wyn ap Hugh (q.v.) was one of his receivers. In September of that year, the pirate Captain Sergeant arrived at St Tudwal's isle with two prizes laden with corn. One of the ships, complete with

cargo, was bought openly by John Roberts of Caernarfon. John Griffiths of Llŷn took eight men and seized the 'pirate goods' from Roberts in the name of the Queen and the Lord Admiral.

## THE LEGEND OF CAPTAIN JONES

A book printed in 1631 and 1659 was attributed to Montgomeryshire's David Lloyd (1597-1663), but is sometimes attributed to Martin Lluelyn (1616-1682) and/or William Marshall (fl. 1617-1650). The 1671 frontispiece (E. Okes and Francis Haley, London printers) reads as follows:

*The Legend of Captain Jones:*

*Relating to his Adventure to sea, his First Landing, and Strange Combat with a Mighty Bear: His Furious Battel with his six and thirty Men, against the Army of Eleven Kings, with their Overthrow and deaths: His Relieving of Kemper* [Quimper] *Castle: His Strange and Admirable Sea-Fight with Six Huge Gallies of Spain, and nine thousand Soldiers: His being taken Prisoner, and Hard Usage: Lastly, His being set at Liberty by the King's Command, and Return for England.*

Jones is apparently a historical figure,

recounted in the above entry, and his exploits are the stuff of legend in this verse ballad, but the author has not been able to source a copy of the book for further research. There is a copy available from a USA rare books website at $1,000, but it has been downloaded on the web. The work is a verse satire on the legend of Captain John Smith of *Pocahontas* fame.

## JOHN CALLICE (CALLYS, CALLIS)
## fl. 1571-1587
*'The most famous English* [sic] *pirate of the 16th century', 'The Most Dangerous Pyrate in the Realm'*

Gosse wrote in 1932 that John Callys was *'like many of his profession a man of birth and education. Among his relatives was the Earl of Pembroke, one of the leading peers of the realm. Callys first sailed as an officer of the Royal Navy under Sir John Berkeley, but afterwards turned pirate.'* Callice went on to loot ships in the Bristol Channel, the Scilly Islands, East Anglia, Scotland, the North Sea and the Barbary Coast. He moved to London aged eleven, to be apprenticed to Alderman Bounds as a haberdasher, and he then became a merchant, supplying the ships in the Pool

*Gatehouse at Cefnamwlch, home of the Griffiths family*

of London. Callice may well have been 'pressed' when he joined the Royal Navy in 1571, sailing first with Sir William Winter, and then under Sir John Berkeley.

However, by 1574 he was operating as a pirate, captaining the *Cost Me Noughte*. A kinsman of the Earl of Pembroke, Callice built upon his connections with the Glamorgan gentry, and was an intimate friend of the Comptroller and Serjeant of the Admiralty at Cardiff, even staying at the serjeant's house when he came ashore. Callice also is known to have stayed with William Herbert and with Sir John Perrot's agent at Haverfordwest. Nevertheless, the Lords of the Admiralty referred to him as '*a notorious pyrate haunting the coasts of Wales*', and Callice was the unofficial leader of a bunch of pirate captains such as his cronies Robert Hickes and 'Brother Battes'.

By early 1574, he was master of *Oliphant* (Elephant), a royal ship, and took an Italian merchantman, the *Grace of God*, owned by Acerbo Velutelli, selling her cargo in Cardiff and Bristol. The heavily-armed ship was owned by the courtier Sir Henry Knollys and '*appears to have been full of pirates.*' Fernando Fielding was captain and Simao Fernandes the Portuguese pilot. In December, a rich Portuguese ship was taken off the Azores, with sugar and exotic hardwoods. The Portuguese ambassador alleged that Fernandes had personally killed seven Portuguese seamen, but he was never charged. Later, in court in 1577, Callice stated that Fielding had sold him the ship for one hundred guineas, even though Knollys was the rightful owner. It seems that Callice was protecting Knollys' reputation in court. Callice then captained the *Oliphant* until at least February 1576, but was captaining other ships from November of that year.

Sir John Perrot (q.v.) was also a friend of Callice and his accomplice Hickes. Callice sold the *Elephant* to his pirate friend Robert Hickes around 1575. In 1576 Callice and Battes brought into Cardiff *Our Lady of the Conception*, a Spanish vessel laden with wool consigned to merchants in Bruges. The merchants complained to the Admiralty, which sent a man with orders to recover the wool from its receivers in Cardiff. However, we read of '*William Herbert of the High Street, and*

*Robert ap Ifan disobeying process of the Court of Admiralty and misusing him that came with that process.*' Callice had sailed around the coast of Wales to Denbigh, where he sold the remains of the wool. The Lord Admiral reported to the Council that he '*was otherwise a notorious malefactor and had committed sundry great piracies*'. Certain dignitaries in Cardiff and Glamorgan, including the Sheriff, were ordered to London to explain their actions in not arresting Callice.

From 1574 to 1577 Callice had plundered anything that moved, especially in the Bristol Channel and off the South Coast of England, and several other captains joined his fleet, attracted by his success and the ineptitude and corruption of the authorities. From Holy Island to Yarmouth, and the Scillies to Lundy he was known, and was master of the Bristol Channel. Cardiff was a particular centre for smuggling and piracy, probably because the powerful Herbert family controlled most of Glamorgan and south-east Wales. In south-east Wales, the Herbert Earls of Worcester, later to become the Earls of Pembroke, replicated Sir John Perrot's power-base in south-west Wales (see Walter Herbert and Morgan Matthew, above). Callice was free to move around Cardiff and dispose of his goods at will, because of his connections with the Herbert family.

Callice took major prizes from Denmark to the Azores, as well as off Cornwall and France. Simao Fernandes bought a small barque from William Herbert, Vice-Admiral of Wales, and joined with Callice's *Oliphant* in April 1576. They jointly took a Portuguese caravel off the Canary Isles.

The Privy Council now assessed Callice as '*the most dangerous pyrate in the realm*', and pirates such as Heynes, Hickes, Bates, the Dutch Counte Higgenberte and the Portuguese Simon Fernandino acknowledged him as their leader. Gosse refers to Callice generally sailing alone, '*but sometimes joined forces with two foreign corsairs, Count Higgenberte and Symon Ferdinando Portingale* [Portuguese]*, or else with his old friend Captain Robert Hickes of Saltash, who was afterwards hanged.*' At this time Captain Gregory Penry of Tenby 'made no merchant's voyages by a long time, but hath kept the seas, taking and spoiling such things as he could meet withall'. However, Fernandes was gaoled in May 1576 by South Wales Admiralty officials. He had claimed that he had made no profits from the Portuguese caravel, so his backers turned against him. However, after a few months, William Herbert paid his bail, and the charges were dropped. Fernandes stayed in Cardiff, protected by Herbert, but the Portuguese sued to recover their goods. Callice used Poole and Lulworth Cove in the West Country, and brought into Cornwall the French *L'Esperance* in 1576 with its cargo of Gascony wine. He also took into Penarth Roads a homecoming Breton ship laden with Newfoundland cod which he had taken in the Straits of Belle Île off Brittany.

Many Bristol Channel pirates were hanged in the late 1570's, including 'Brother Battes'. The Bristol Channel pirates were nationally known, with captains Battes, Hicks, Fielding, Ward, Purser, William Chick and Tom Clarke being among the most prominent, operating from Cornwall to Cardiff, and from Pembroke to the east coast of Ireland. Prizes were brought into the shelter of Penarth Roads and goods transferred to Cardiff merchants. In North

*Old Point House, Angle, Pembrokeshire was cut off by the tide and used by Callice and other pirates*

Wales, Bardsey (Enlli) and St Tudwal's islands were notable pirate haunts. The government was so annoyed with local officials in Wales that in 1576 it appointed a special Admiralty Commissioner, John Croft, to investigate why Callice was allowed to roam free. Croft arrested Robert Fresher in Cardiff, amongst Callice's *'aiders and retainers'* there. He then received intelligence that Callice had just left Cardiff for Newport and then to Penarth Roads, but Frost failed to receive support from the Mayor and Corporation of Bristol to arrest Callice.

On his return to Cardiff he wrote in 1576 *'I required aide there for the apprehending of Callis' prize but I colde have none, nor any willingness offred me therein, althoughe in speche every sorte of people colde saie it were wll donne to take them; and there I founde certen knowledge that the Townesmen of Cardiffe and sondry gentlemen thereabouts did comonly buy and receave divers of the goods and spoiles brought there by Callis and his compplices, and gave them aide with victualles and other necessaries.'*

In December 1576 Croft discovered that Callice had returned to Cardiff with a stolen boat carrying *'sammon herrings and Manchester kersies'*, with its crew *'kept as prisoner under the hatches'*. The Vice-Admiral of Monmouth, Sir William Morgan of Llantarnam, Newport, sent a crew to pay Callice, and took the prize to Newport. Morgan's crew refused to deal with Croft, who reported one man *'did not only utterly refuse to aid me but also obstinately did say that he did not care for the commission or me.'* Morgan's men carried on unloading the cargo, while the imprisoned crew called out from the holds for water and food. Croft implored the local JP's William Morgan of Llantarnam and Rowland Morgan of Machen to help in arresting the pirates, but they refused to act. The Privy Council later took no action against these magistrates, although Callice soon took some French ships and a Danish ship. Under the pseudonym of Kanter, he boarded and took a ship in Helford Haven. After the Herberts, the Morgans were the most powerful family in these parts, and were linked by marriage to the Herberts.

In fact, the well-known pirate 'Brother Battes' was a friend of William Morgan, and William Thickyns confessed the following dealings at Milord Haven: *'Battes had a ship of 160 tons and lay there with nothing in her but men and ordinance. He this deponent fell to practise with Captain Battes, first whether he should go with this deponent into Barbary upon certain good occasions, which this deponent did disclose to him, and he said yea with all his heart ... and he said he would go with this examinant, but for all his former contracts with William Morgan Knight, who was so worshipful a gentleman that he could not find it in his heart to break his words to him.*' Morgan was one of the Vice-Admirals of Wales, governor of Dungarvan, Marshall in Ireland, and had recently bought 634 'elephants' teeth' (tusks) off Battes.

Fernandes was again arrested in February 1577, but released by Thomas Lewes, the Cardiff magistrate and a well-known conduit for pirate loot. A 1577 letter from a Haverfordwest JP to Sir John Perrot reads '*Cardiff is the general resort of pyrates and there they are sheltered and protected*'. Nicholas Herbert was Sheriff of Glamorgan at that time, and was a definite accomplice of pirates. Callice next took Peter Chamberlain's salt sloop, transferring to her 28 '*pieces of ordinance*', fitting her out as his ship, and disposing of the cargo and fittings along the ports of Pembrokeshire. Already the Privy Council had complained to Sir John Perrot (q.v.) about piracy in Pembrokeshire, on January 12th, 1577:

'*Whereas their Lordships are given to understand that one John Callice, a notable pyrate frequenting that country and arriving lately at Milford, was lodged and housed at Haverfordwest, and being there was suffered to escape, their Lordships do not a little marvel at the negligence of such that are Justices in those parts that knowing the said Callice to be so notable an offender would suffer him to depart in that order.*' The local authorities had, however, '*for a show and colour of justice... apprehended some of the poorest and permitted the chiefest pyrates to depart*', as they had put six of Callice's crew in gaol. The local authorities put the blame for Callice's 'escape' upon their counterparts in Cardiff.

Callice seemed to have spent some time at the Old Point House in Angle, Pembroke, now a fascinating pub sometimes cut off by the tide, and with a fire which has not gone out for hundreds of years. George Owen wrote of Caldey Island at this time that it was '*very fertile and yieldeth plenty of corn all their ploughs* give with horses, for oxen the inhabitants dare not keep fearing the purveyors of the pirates.' Robert Hickes sailed to again join up with Callice in February 1577, and Callice took over command of his ship. They took three Scottish and a German ship off southern England. They then headed north to link up with William Fenner's heavily-armed pinnace, and on 12 April 1577 off Beachy Head, captured the 300-ton Danish 8-gun ship *Golden Lion* of Elsinore. Fifteen Danish seamen were badly wounded. After the ship's capture, its Captain, Pieterson, lay '*maimed in his left leg with a musket shot*'. He was '*threatened to be tormented*', i.e. tortured if he refused to tell Callice where the cash on board, around £100, was hidden. Indeed, the French ambassador complained to Walsingham that Callice '*tortured the men and mariners with extraordinary cruelties*'. The prize was sailed to Weymouth for the cargo to be sold.

However, Callice was finally captured on May 15th, 1577, by Edward Horsey, the Captain of the Isle of Wight. On his person was found the enormous sum of £22 and 7 shillings, which was later offered as a piece of incriminating evidence at his trial. Callice was conveyed to London '*under sure guard*' and lodged in the Tower of London, awaiting trial by Dr Lewis of Abergavenny, Judge of the Admiralty. Callice was interrogated by Dr Lewis in the Winchelsea Prison, and insisted upon being called a gentleman, although he could not read or sign his name. His only possessions were those worth £10 a year at Tintern, which he had not seen since he was 11 years old. In 1577 the pirate leader William Chick was also captured and turned informer when threatened with the thumbscrew and rack. Both Callice and Chick incriminated Nicholas Herbert, Sheriff of Glamorgan (and John Callice's father-in-law!); William Herbert, the former Mayor of Cardiff; Edward Kemeys of Cefn Mably Manor; and John Thomas Fleming of Flemingston. They did not suffer the same fate as the lesser pirates, of course.

Callice knew all the corrupt officials in South Wales, and usually disposed of his goods through Cardiff. Robert Hickes took more ships in 1577, and hearing of Callice's capture, offered in a letter to surrender the *Golden Lion* (now renamed the *Neptune*), in return for the release of Callice. The pirate Robert Hickes of Saltash wrote, desiring that they would meet again: *'Brother Callys... If all I have of mine own to my shirt, may stand you in stead you shall as fair command it as my brother born ... wherefore I pray you send me word either by mouth or pen what you will wish me to do for you ... I will do it if the surrendering of the ship may by any means gain your liberty ... Fare you well and I pray God send us both our hearts and a merry meeting.'* However,

*Caldey was often used for revictualling pirate ships*

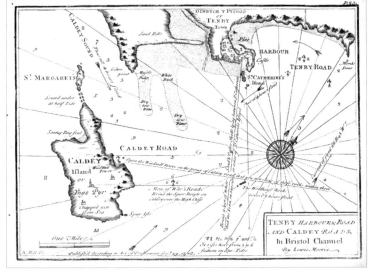

Hickes was captured in October 1577 and hung in chains in 1578 at Wapping Dock, after a trial by the Admiralty Court in London. Trial records show that he swindled Callice out of his share of the booty. Brother Battes was also hung in this year, presumably following Callice's disclosures.

Callice had powerful friends. David Lewis, Judge of the High Court of the Admiralty, stated that influential men in Wales would not arrest a source of their profits – but *'will play bo-peep, seest me and seest me not.'* Vice-Admiral Sir William Morgan deliberately refused to help his local piracy commission. The Earl of Pembroke's Herbert family held the port of Cardiff, and the 'arch-pirate' John Callice used to lodge with the High Sheriff of Glamorgan when he docked at Cardiff.

The sheriff was Callice's father-in-law, and the controller and customs and the Admiralty port-sergeant were Herbert appointees. Callice had been safe there. The Clerk to the Council of Wales and the Marches sent to Cardiff to buy Callice's plundered salt. The Mayor of Cardiff, Thomas Lewis, had also bought goods from Callice and his colleagues. Callice was charged with six major acts of piracy and many minor ones, and sentenced to hang. He was called '*a notorious malefactor who hath committed sundry great piracies*'.

The pirate had no wish to hang in chains, so turned Queen's Evidence, his petition to the Queen reading '*I bewail my former wicked life, and beseech God and her Majesty to forgive me ... If she will only spare my life and use me in her service by sea and with those she can best trust, either to clear the coast of other wicked pyrates or otherwise, as I know their haunts, roads and maintainers so well, I can do more therein than if she sent ships abroad and spent £20,000. I send herewith particulars of the partakers of my pyracies and the maintainers of and victuallers of me and my companions.*' Callice gave a list of his supporters and '*receivers*', including Thomas Lewis of the Van in Bedwas, and among his creditors was the deputy Vice-Admiral of South Wales. While the judges

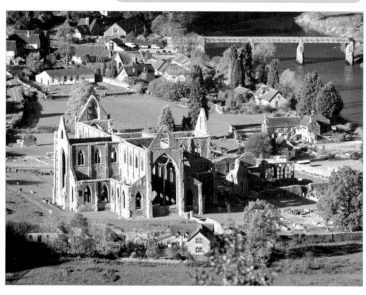

*Tintern Abbey and village*

were deciding whether to execute him, the Regent of Scotland, Earl Morton, offered £500 for Callice's release, and the influence of several powerful men assisted his cause. Callice also gave evidence against his receivers, and had written to Lord Walsingham to say that if he was spared, he would help rid the coast of pirates by giving particulars of their '*roads, haunts, creeks and maintainers*'. Among the 'maintainers', or receivers of smuggled and pirated goods was Lord O'Sullivan of Berehaven.

Sir Francis Walsingham, the head of the secret service, ensured that Callice was released on a technicality. He needed Callice to exploit the Portuguese Fernandes' knowledge of the Caribbean and American coasts, for an expedition he was planning with Humphrey Gilbert. Callice was released on parole on 14 July 1578, but quickly fled his parole officer to be commissioned to take part in Sir Humphrey Gilbert's voyage to the Americas alongside the young Walter Raleigh. He again became the *Elephant's* pilot for his old comrade Sir Henry Knollys. The *Elephant* was Knollys' flagship of his three ships, and Fernando Fielding also was on the ship as a 'soldier-gentleman'. Humphrey Gilbert assembled his fleet at Plymouth, but the *Elephant* carried on her privateering ways of the previous four years. Knollys and Callice defeated the pirate Robert Holbourne, capturing his ship and its French prize. They were stripped of booty, and Holbourne was released back in Plymouth. Knollys' other two ships were also practising piracy, so Humphrey Gilbert argued with Knollys. Knollys and Callice promptly took their small flotilla to Ireland and the Isle of Wight, taking another French ship.

Gilbert's great expedition thus broke up, and Knollys was investigated for his crimes in 1579, but no charges were laid. His sister was married to the queen's favourite, the Earl of Essex. Walter Raleigh was due to captain the *Falcon* on the expedition, with Callice's associate Simao Fernandes as his lieutenant. Fernandes and Raleigh took a prize off the Cape Verde Islands, and Fernandes was Raleigh's pilot to the Americas in 1584, 1585 and 1587, serving also under Frobisher in 1588 against the Spanish Armada.

When one of Raleigh's captains took a

French prize, it was turned over to John Callice, who returned it to its owners but kept the cargo. Raleigh took some of the booty, but most was smuggled ashore by Sir George Carey (the brother-in-law of Lord Admiral Thomas Howard) in Hampshire, where he was Vice-Admiral, in charge of customs. When the French owners sued in the Admiralty Court, they lost because Callice and Carey had bribed the chief judge, Julius Caesar. As usual, Callice had powerful friends. Carey was a kinsman of Queen Elizabeth, who became Baron Hunsdon and embezzled huge amounts of money as treasurer for the Irish Wars.

The Admiralty Court awarded the owners of Callice's French prize £4,000 in 1579, but Callice made no payment. (In modern times this would represent about £1 million). However, it appears that he did make a payment of around £505 to the owners of the 1576 Danish prize taken by him, Hickes and William Fenner, the *Golden Lion*. Callice took two ships off Hamburg in 1580, probably still funded by Knollys, and made his base again in South Wales. In 1582, William Fenner gained a commission to pursue pirates, and in August promptly hired his old colleague Callice as lieutenant, who quickly took several

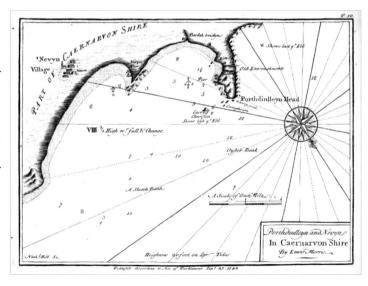

merchant vessels. The 100-ton 'Gallion Fenner' of Chichester had a crew of 70 in 1582, probably three times as many as an equivalent merchantman, and twice as many as a naval vessel. After Fenner, Callice was in command, followed by the master (an expert seaman and 'lodesman'), then the owner, Edward Fenner. (Edward was a landlubber, so had little authority at sea). Next in the pecking order of command were the gunner, the master's mate, the boatswain and the purser, the gunner's mate, the boatswain's mate, the cook and his mate, the shipwright, six soldiers, three quartermasters and then 45 general hands, each of whom was assigned a specified number of shares in any loot taken.

In March 1583 Callice took two Scottish ships and sold their cargo at Plymouth. He kept one of the Scottish ships, the *Falcon* of Prestonpans and renamed it the *Golden Chalice*, but abandoned her to prevent his arrest. (Sir Humphrey Gilbert used her on his 1583 Newfoundland Expedition). On board the

*Porthdinllaen was a well-known haunt isolated for pirates and smugglers to trade*

*Falcon* were two packs of religious books for James VI, which Callice sold for £40 to the Huguenot printer Vautrollier. In 1584, William Fenner was granted an extension to his privateering licence, to take Spanish and Portuguese prizes, and Callice again became his lieutenant on the *Gallion Fenner*, with 70 crew. Fenner's nephew Edward, the brother of Captain George Fenner, joined and in December they took a French warship. Callice was made captain of the prize. More ships were taken, mainly French, but also including a Portuguese sugar drover. In 1584, Peter Chamberlain, whose salt sloop had been taken by Callice eight years earlier, complained to the Admiralty that he had been robbed at sea '*by Count Helleburg and John Callice, pyrates.*' William and Edward Fenner were arrested in 1585, after they had separated from Callice in stormy weather, but were never convicted.

Edward and William both captained ships against the Armada, and William died during Drake's 1590 raid on Lisbon. Callice was later arrested in Ireland, but seems to have escaped again, capturing several French ships. However, Callice was now finding that his main areas of operations, the Bristol Channel and Ireland were becoming more difficult to trade in, and he was still being chased for the 1579 £4,000 judgement. Callice sometime in 1586 was pirating in the Orkneys, but lost his ship and all his belongings. He was thus reduced to serving as a seaman on the *Minikin*, a pirate ship owned by a Mr Bellingham. He practised piracy off the Barbary Coast, and was probably killed in 1586 or 1587. According to Captain John Smith, the founder of Virginia (and of *Pocahontas* fame), '*this ancient pirate Collis, who most refreshed himself upon the coast of Wales... grew famous till Queen Elizabeth of Blessed Memory hanged him at Wapping*', but he died in a sea engagement after he joined the Barbary Corsairs. However, Gosse believes that he was hanged with two other active pirates off the coast of Wales, captains Pursser and Clinton.

## CAPTAIN HENRY ROBERTS
### fl. 1576-1596

In 1576, Roberts was in command of the *Christopher* of Dartmouth, when captured and taken to the Inquisition at Tenerife. '*Howbeit, Captain Roberts, by means of a friar was delivered out of prison (which cost him all the merchandise he brought with him in his ship) and so returned with dead freight to the sum of 200 pound.*' To compensate for this looting, letters of marque were issued to Andrew Barker of Bristol, whose ship it was, and in pursuance of these letters he and Roberts made their famous voyage to the Honduras in 1576. In 1581, Captain Roberts captured two Portuguese barques bound from Brazil, and in 1592 was again in the West Indies at Cavannas Harbour in Havana. His ship was the 140-ton '*Exchange*' of Bristol, and he sailed alongside a fleet owned by Master Watts and under Captain Lane. With other Welshmen, Roberts was on the Somers and Preston expedition to the Indies in 1595, when Porto Santo and Santiago de Leon were taken. Joined by the British privateers *Solomon* and *Jane Bonaventure*, many merchant ships were taken carrying '*sack, canary, muscadel, oil, hides, salsaparilla, indigo and balsamum*'. Captain John Myddelton (q.v.) was also in Captain Roberts' company at Havana. According to Robert Davie, Roberts was commanding the *Derling* when killed at Jamaica on a secret mission in 1596.

## WELSH BUCCANEERS UNDER SIR FRANCIS DRAKE 1585-1595

In Drake's great voyage of 1585, sacking Santiago, San Domingo, Cartagena and St Augustine, his Sergeant Major was Anthony Powell, his Captain Matthew Morgan, and Captain Robert Pugh was one of his two '*corporals of the field*'. Morgan led the vanguard at San Domingo and the rear-guard at Cartagena, where Powell carried out the main attack, carrying the barricades in a terrific frontal charge: '*We soon found out the barricades of pipes and butts to be the meetest* [most suitable] *place for our assault, which, notwithstanding it was well furnished with pikes and shot, was, without staying, straightway attempted by us. Down went the butts of earth, and pell-mell came our swords and pikes together after our shot had first given their volley even at the enemy's nose.*' Powell died after leading the attack on St John's Fort in Florida, shot while chasing the fleeing Spaniards. In Drake's last voyage of 1595, Lieutenant Jones was killed by hostile Indians and Maurice Williams, '*one of her majesty's guard*', was killed during the march on Panama.

## A Note upon 16th century Welsh Piracy

The death of Henry VIII in 1547 had stimulated the rise of piracy. His widow's brother-in-law, Thomas Seymour was Lord High Admiral, and took half of what was looted, even seizing the Scilly Isles for himself. He attempted to marry Elizabeth Tudor, and under his rule the Admiralty Courts did not persecute pirates. From the 1550's to the 1570's, no pirate vessel had been taken while unloading cargo, in the secret and immune ports of Wales and the West Country. It seems that the pirates usually took around a fifth of the proceeds, with the receivers, who had support of the local lords, took 80%, which was 'dispersed' easily into the surrounding countryside. There were no warships on the Irish Sea, and no regular patrols off the Welsh coast. The official guardship of the Vice-Admiral, the '*Flying Hart*', was based at Newport until it was plundered by pirates in 1578.

No pirate was taken at sea, and no prominent pirate ever arrested in Pembroke or Cornwall. Port officials turned a blind eye, or participated in piracy. Certain pirates who anchored in the Penarth Roads actually stayed with the local 'serjeant of the Admiralty'. The building up of British sea power, culminating in the defeat of the Armada in 1588, meant that by the 1590's, piracy in the Bristol Channel was virtually suppressed. Pirates increasingly operated away from the British Isles, but outbreaks flared up until 1630. In that year Charles I tried to requisition a 30-ton barque with crew and provisions from the County of Glamorgan, but the local justices responded that not even Cardiff possessed a pinnace of that size. The only five ships that big had been captured by Moorish pirates, while taking Welsh butter to France and Ireland.

Callice's arrest was followed by a 'round-up' of Cardiff pirates in 1577. Hickes and Battes were hung, and Callice imprisoned, as London finally began to deal with the worst area for piracy in the whole of the kingdom. In March 1577, partly because of Callice's confessions, the Vice-President of Wales and the Marches was ordered by Elizabeth to appoint a strong commission to investigate '*certain disorders committed by pyrates*' in Glamorgan and Monmouthshire. This was a real warning to her half-brother, Sir John Perrot, in south-west Wales. The commissioners, Sir John Perrot, Fabian Phillips and Thomas Lewis, Mayor of Cardiff, were expressly desired by the Privy Council '*to take some pains therein*'. By April 3rd, Phillips and Lewis could report to the Council that they had examined up to sixty suspected pirates and their retainers in Cardiff. They doubted the integrity and commitment of Perrot, and complained of his frequent absences. They also tried to convict Nicholas Herbert, Sheriff of Glamorgan. Upon being summoned to appear, he refused on the excuse that he had to be present at the Easter Assizes. Upon being informed, the Privy Council told him to attend the assizes and then travel directly to London to answer the charges brought against him.

The transgressors, led by Herbert, made a legal challenge '*for that in matters of spoils done on sea and what concerneth persons accessory by land there seemeth to be a difference in law.*' However, in June the Privy Council ordered the Judge of the Admiralty to consult with the Attorney General and Solicitor-General, to ascertain the legal situation and call for new legislation if necessary. Lord Walsingham also wrote in June to the Attorney General '*to hasten his answer to the Council touching the fittest means to punish the aiders of pyrates about Cardiff.*' Many of the Cardiff transgressors were forced to travel to see the Privy Council, and in early 1578 the six ringleaders, including the Sheriff of Glamorgan, were fined between £10 and £20 and bound over not to repeat their crimes.

## SIR JOHN PERROT
### 1527-1592 – *the Son of Henry VIII*
Henry VIII had an illegitimate son by one of the royal ladies-in-waiting, Mary Berkeley. She married Thomas Perrot, of Haroldston near Haverfordwest, who was knighted as a 'reward' for the marriage. John Perrot was born at Haroldston, educated at St David's, and entered the household of the Marquis of Winchester. He was given massive estates in Pembrokeshire by his father, the king. Edward VI, Mary and Elizabeth I all acknowledged John Perrot as a half-brother, a giant of a man, he strongly resembled his father. Henry VIII offered John a preferment, but the king died before he could award it, and John was a great friend of Edward VI, who made him a Knight of the Bath. In 1554, at a tournament for his half-sister Queen Mary Tudor and her husband Philip of Spain, he '*fought best of all*' of the Spanish and English grandees. Mary herself gave out the prizes, including '*a diamond ring of great value*'. However, he was denounced for his strong Protestantism and was imprisoned by Mary for a short time in the Fleet prison, before going overseas to serve under his friend the Earl of Pembroke. He returned when he knew that Mary was dying.

Sir John was one of the four knights who carried Elizabeth I's canopy at her coronation, and was her great favourite. As early as 1547, the 20 year-old Sir John Perrot was petitioned by John David to the effect that '*pyrates (it is commonly reported) are furnished, victualled, aided, received and succoured – all their goods openly sold in Cardiff.*' In 1552, Sir John as Vice-Admiral was ordered by the Lordships of the Admiralty to send up to London one Phillip ap Rice, a pirate '*whom he and others in that countrie supporteth*'. There had been frequent reports of this Welsh pirate attacking shipping in the Bristol Channel, in consort with a Spaniard, John de Andreaca. To conceal his business with Phillip ap Rice, instead Perrot promptly arrested William Rogers of Herefordshire and Captain Thomas Harys, who had plundered ten Flemish ships, and sought a haven in Pembrokeshire.

In 1554, the Admiralty asked Perrot to chase the pirate Captain Jones, and then in 1556 ordered the Sheriff of Pembroke to come to London, to explain why he had not arrested the pirates Peter Heall and William ap Rees of Sandy Haven; William ap Rees of Haverfordwest; and Philip ap Rees of Pyll. In 1555, 'Jones the Pirate' took a Breton ship and brought it into Tenby to dispose of. Also in 1555, when pirates brought a captured ship into Tenby, Sir John Morgan, a former Sheriff of Pembrokeshire

arrested the crew, but sold the cargo for his own profit. Presumably Perrot had his share. In 1556, Merrick Morgan was busy attacking ships off the Pembroke coast, while Sir John turned a blind eye.

Perrot was reprimanded in 1564 when 'certain of Thomas Cobham's company stayed at Tenby', and the pirates stayed free because of the 'marvellous insufficiency' of Perrot's deputy at Tenby. Cobham had seized the Spanish ship *Santa*

*Catarina*, which became a major international incident involving Phillip II of Spain. The situation was complicated for Sir John, as Thomas Cobham was the brother of Lord Cobham, Warden of the Ports. Perrot was dismissed from his post as Vice-Admiral of Wales in 1565 because of the corruption of his deputies in dealing with piracy, and his name omitted from the Pembrokeshire Piracy Commission.

Perrot had made vast wealth from being Vice-Admiral for the coast of South and West Wales, much from collusion with pirates, built a great manor at Haroldston, and rebuilt Laugharne and Carew castles as manor houses. The harbour of Laugharne was noted as being safe for pirates to unload cargo at night. Haverfordwest, Tenby and Cardigan were also used by pirates, who stayed with Sir John's agents. Perrot was still MP for Pembrokeshire, and Mayor of Haverfordwest.

Queen Elizabeth next appointed him first Lord President of Munster in 1571, to suppress the Fitzmaurice Rebellion there,

*Laugharne castle was rebuilt as a Manor House by Sir John Perrot, who collaborated with pirates*

which he did within a year. From 1573, Perot was engaged in much litigation to increase his lands, having returned to Wales to lead '*a countryman's life*', as he informed his fellow-Welshman Lord Burghley. From 1574, as a member of the Council for Wales and the Marches, he was supposed to be actively involved in the suppression of piracy, and in 1575 made chief commissioner to suppress piracy in Pembrokeshire. He now made a pretence of appearing to act against pirates, proclaiming his intentions and imprisoning one of his own men for a short time in (comfortable) captivity at Pembroke. At the same time Robert Hickes, the accomplice of John Callice, was selling stolen corn openly from his ship the *Jonas* to the Mayor of Pembroke and respectable merchantmen.

Perrot acted against Scottish smugglers, but actively encouraged piracy, while including in his reports to Whitehall incidents where he had 'accidentally' purchased illegal goods, as a defence against any informers. In 1576, he refused to take over a similar post for Glamorgan and Monmouthshire. A bitter feud had developed between Perrot and Richard

Vaughan, chief commissioner for piracy in Carmarthenshire. Captain Hickes, already noted in the entry upon John Callice, had captured the *Jonas*, bound from Konigsberg to Lisbon with a cargo of corn, near Land's End. Hickes brought his prize into Milford Haven, and began to sell the corn, and also a cargo of salt which had previously been looted.

Hickes dealt for five weeks with the whole spectrum of West Wales society, from a priest named Andrew who was buying enough corn for the winter, to George Devereux, uncle of the Earl of Essex, who bought 200 barrels of rye to illegally export to Spain. Perrot sent an unliveried retainer aboard to help Hickes keep account of his sales. The Mayor of Pembroke bought some corn and sent it in his ship the *Maudlen* to Galicia to offload. Another local vessel, the *George*, took corn to Portugal.

Vice-Admiral Vaughan and Perrot both blamed the other. Perrot seems to have taken the biggest bribes, but also covered his tracks well, as he had made a record of Vaughan's trips to see Hickes. Vaughan had seen the opportunity for advancement as a pirate-catcher. His first move was to go aboard Hickes' ship to haggle for a bribe, to avert suspicion. He then corresponded with Sir William Morgan of Abergavenny, the Vice-Admiral for South Wales, suggesting that Morgan send a warship, or come in his own *Flying Hart* to take the pirate ship. (A few months later the *Flying Hart* was plundered by pirates as it lay at Newport). However, Morgan declined to do anything. Vaughan recruited retainers at great expense from south-east Wales, as he know most Pembroke men were loyal to Perrot, and twenty of his confederates were sent aboard Hickes' ship on the pretext of trafficking. Their watchword for the assault was to be '*he that is a friend unto John Callice, stand unto me!*'

However, Perrott had become increasingly uneasy about the constant traffic in the Haven between his supporters and Hickes. At the end of five weeks, he exploded into a rage while watching from an overlooking hill. He issued warrants to his servants to put an end to the trade, and tell Hickes to make his way out of Milford Haven. He may have received word that Morgan had been contacted by Vaughan, and was fearing the arrival of a naval vessel in his domain. Next to Hickes' ship was a pinnace loaded with 40 tons of wheat, which was Vaughan's bribe, and Sir John's men sailed it away. This alarmed Hickes' men, and all sixty of them quickly armed and prepared for action. Vaughan's men swiftly called off their plan, leaving Vaughan fuming. He had lost his bribe, his pirate and his glory. Hickes now began stripping the *Jonas*, '*not leaving a piece of rope the length of an arm*', transferring everything to his own ship.

Hickes intended to burn the ship, but the merchantman's Captain Rung protested, and bribed Vaughan to intercede. Rung sold the bare hulk to Perrot for just £10, enough for him and his crew to return to London. However, a French captive from the *Jonas*, Louis Bourdain of St Malo, was given to Sir John by Hickes as a 'present' before he sailed off. Bourdain was sent to Little Newcastle (the birthplace of Black Bart Roberts) and ransomed. The Frenchman managed to escape as far as Swansea, but Sir William Herbert returned him to his cousin Sir John, and Bourdain was thrown into Carew Castle. He was fed only on a diet of dried fish and bread. 200 crowns was offered for him by his mother, and a Chester merchant creditor of Bourdain's offered £100. Perrot held out for a cargo of Gascony wine, and at great expense, Bourdain's brothers sent a cargo. However, before the ship reached Tenby, Bourdain had escaped again and was harboured by some of Vaughan's men at Pendine. Vaughan managed to take for himself 10 tuns of the Gascon wine, which was possibly his only victory in his dealing with Sir John. Poor Bourdain reached Cardiff, where he fell into the clutches of his Chester creditor.

The feud between the two local magnates grew, and in 1577 Vaughan tried to board a ship belonging to Davy Allen of Laugharne, lying off Laugharne, Perrot's private beach, with cargo for Perrot. He had ridden from Whitland on the advice of an informer that the boat was full of '*both murtherers and thieves*', and rowed up to the ship, demanding to know its cargo. The crew yelled back '*that you shall not know, for none have to do here but Sir John Perrot.*' Vaughan noted ten men '*with culvers ready with fire in their cocks*' (i.e. ready to fire) and rowed away quickly. There were also two ships wrecked on

Pendine Sands in a storm, and Sir John's men began collecting booty before Vaughan arrived with a fleet of 60 men in small boats from Tenby. After a squabble, Vaughan's men were forced to give up anything that they gathered off the wrecks. Vaughan himself had acquired two brass cannon and several bags of spice, which were '*confiscated*' by Perrot's followers, leaving Vaughan with '*nothing but shame and repulse.*' The famed Huguenot privateer Luke Ward, sailing under the flag of the Prince of Conde, put into Milford Haven with a prize, and was arrested by Vaughan, but Perrot released the privateers.

Richard Vaughan lodged a bill of complaint against Perrot in Privy Council, and told crowds outside the Blue Boar in Holborn that '*Sir John better deserved hanging than any thief.*' His bill was found to be so malicious that Vaughan was imprisoned and deprived of office in 1578. Perrot once again 'campaigned' against pirates as far as The Needles. However, he visited his friends at Falmouth during this voyage, the noted Killigrew pirate family. There are many examples of Perrot supporting piracy. The first record of piracy in and around Newfoundland took place in 1582 when Sir John Perrot and Henry Oughtred launched a raid on Portuguese and Spanish fishermen around the Avalon Peninsula. To protect their vessels from these and other ships, Basque fish merchants began to apply for passports from the Lord Admiral of England.

Perrot was then appointed by Elizabeth Lord Deputy of Ireland from 1584 to 1588, but was arrested on a false charge of treason in 1591 and sentenced to death. Perrot's comments about his half-sister were reckless. She had appointed a Mr Errington to be clerk of the Exchequer in Ireland, and Sir John exclaimed '*this fiddling woman troubles me out of measure. God's dear Lady, he shall not have the office! I will give it to Sir Thomas Williams!*' Again, at the time of the Spanish Invasion of 1588, he was reported to have said '*Ah silly woman, now she will not curb me! Now she shall not rule me! Now, God's dear Lady, I shall be her white boy again!*' He added, when Sir John Garland brought him a letter from the Queen, '*This it is, to serve a base-born woman! Had I served any price in Christendom, I had not been thus dealt with!*' When told he must die, he exclaimed

*'God's death! Will my sister sacrifice her brother to his frisking adversaries?'*

Queen Elizabeth refused to sign the death warrant of her half-brother and planned to pardon him, but he died in 1592 in the Tower of London, aged 65. His main accuser in his tribulations had been Sir Christopher Hatton, a powerful courtier, whose daughter Elizabeth had been seduced by Perrot. Despite his attainder, Perrot's vast estates were granted to his son, Sir Thomas Perrot. John's illegitimate son Sir James Perrot (1571-1630) was a literary man, who became an MP and Vice-admiral for Pembroke, suppressed piracy and wreckers, and was a founder member of the Virginia Company. This author appeared on a RTE documentary charting the descendants of John Perrot to Des Perrot of Cork, who has a far better claim to the kingship of England than the present occupants. (Georg Ludwig, Elector of Hanover, was 57th in line to succeed, but the first Protestant, qualifying as George I of England by his marriage to his cousin, a grand-daughter of James 1. This progenitor of the present royal family was known as *'pig-snout'* in Hanover and his own mother wrote of him and his marriage: *'One hundred thousand thalers a year is a goodly sum to pocket, without speaking of a pretty wife, who will find a match in my son George Louis, the most pigheaded, stubborn boy who ever lived, who has round his brains such a thick crust that I defy any man or woman ever to discover what is in them. He does not care much for the match itself, but one hundred thousand thalers a year have tempted him as they would have tempted anybody else'.* After beating up his 28-year-old wife, Georg imprisoned her for the last thirty years of her life. The new monarchs of Britain always married into Germanic families from George I's accession in 1714 until George VI married Mary Bowes-Lyon and became king in 1936).

**Footnote:**

Caldey, the romantic island just off Tenby, features in the Queen Remembrancer Roll of 1562: *'Caldy, here the pirates are wont many times to victual themselves of sheep and other provisions some times without leave of the owners ... Milford is the great resort and succour of all pirates and enemies in storms whom the country cannot resist.'*

## JOHN WYN AP HUGH (HUW)
### c. 1524-1576

Around the time that Sir John Perrot was actively encouraging piracy in the more prosperous south and south-west of Wales, North Wales was a poor region, which desperately needed income. Around Aberconwy, Nicholas Hookes (q.v.) controlled illicit trade. Hookes and local landowners used Bardsey and St Tudwal islands off the Llŷn peninsula to control illegal trade. Captain George Morgan also operated off the latter around 1565. At the centre of most smuggling and piracy was John Wyn. He was descended from the noble tribe of Collwyn ap Tangno, and bore the royal standard of John Dudley, Earl of Warwick against Kett's Norfolk rebels at Dussindale in 1549. Although unhorsed and wounded, *'yet he upheld the great standard of England'*, and he swiftly rose to prominence, being nominated as Sheriff of Caernarvonshire in the following autumn. (He was a Knight of the Shire from 1552 and also Sheriff in 1559). John Wyn was also granted a 21-year lease of townships and lands in the Llŷn peninsula near the family residence.

Three years later Robert Dudley, Earl of Warwick, had become the Duke of Northumberland, and was licensed to grant John Wyn Bardsey island, and the former abbot of Bardsey's house at Aberdaron. From 1553, John Wyn turned the Augustinian priory on Bardsey (Ynys Enlli – the isle of 40,000 Saints) into a supplies store for pirates. His men on the island were *'at all times ready to deliver to all such pirates ... victuals and necessaries, when and as often as they have need, receiving again of them for the same large recompense as wine, iron, salt, spices ... which the pirates come by their desperate attempts, robbing and spoiling... John Wyn sold goods as far as 80 miles away, and his legal connections ensured that any proceedings against his captains were quietly dropped. He bought corn off the pirate Captain Wolfall, and excused his appearance upon Wolfall's ship to the authorities in 1563, as "Wolfall could speak no Welsh" and needed an interpreter. When searchers went on board, they were prevented from carrying out their duties "for John Wyn ap Hugh and William Glynne declared they had a commission for the like matters, being of more force and authority."'*

In 1567, Morgan ab Ieuan accused John Wyn of using Bardsey isle as the headquarters of a highly-organised nest of pirates. Wyn operated from the old Augustine priory in Bardsey island, and from Beaumaris. One grant was challenged in the court of augmentations by '*upwards of a hundred*' persons, who alleged he had turned them out of their holdings in Bardsey or Aberdaron, and appealed to a prior lease from Henry VIII. It was claimed that 'John ap Wyn' was causing problems for the people, and proceedings against him were instituted in the Court of Star Chamber in 1569. He accused of using Bardsey as a depot for pirates, keeping a factor there to despatch the booty to Chester by sea, and involving his less canny neighbours in prosecutions which he himself evaded as '*a man of good countenance, great power, ability and friendship*' in the county. Wyn was accused of '*being captain, chief and only supporter, defender and maintainor*' of the piracy which was rampant in the area, using Bardsey as his base.

The Bill of Complaint begins: '*the people of Caernarfon have diverse and sundry times heretofore been trouble, molested, vexed, hindered and their great impoverishing and undoing for and by reason certain pyrates,*

*arriving coming for and resorting to those quarters and confines.*' The sufferings were due to '*John Wyn ap Hughe, a man of evil disposition, defender and maintainer of all pyrates... he daily stole ... as well as all kind of beast necessary for victuals, as beefs, steers, wethers and other such like, as also with all kind of meal, bread and other necessaries.*'

He was also charged with selling illicit goods at Chester market aided by his chief assistant and factor, William Morgan. His agent Morgan's duty was to be '*at all times ready to deliver to all such pyrates aforesaid, the said victuals and necessaries, when and as often as they have needs. receiving for the same large recompense – as wine, iron, salt, spices and all such things which the said pyrates by their desperate attempts robbing and spoiling, happen to come by.*' John Wyn always enjoyed the patronage of the powerful Duke of Northumberland who ensured that, despite strenuous efforts by other powerful Welsh families, John Wyn was granted the most influential post of Vice Admiral of North Wales.

The excellent website rhiw.com tells us that '*Morgan ap Ieuan, High Sheriff in 1585 became concerned about the unreasonable behaviour of pirates and smugglers on the* island which he felt was so very alien to the high moral and spiritual standard the island had stood for so many centuries. He brought a serious charge against John Wynn describing him as a terrible man and accused him of being the chief captain, protector and financier of these outlaws, being rewarded with gifts of iron, wine and all kinds of highly saleable goods. He further accused John Wynn of appointing William Morgan, as overseer of the island who aided and encouraged the visits of these lawbreakers by supplying all their needs of water and food and supervising the disposal of the illegal goods to distant markets, like Chester.

This accusation like many others, probably due to John Wynn's influential family came to nothing... There is another example of abuse of power by local dignitaries the case of Sir John Wynn's friend Robert ap Richart who was brought before the court accused of being a pirate. It took but little time

*for Sir John to persuade the six members of the jury that were his tenants of his to find his friend not guilty of any of these foul deeds despite the culprit had pleaded guilty.*' John Wyn's father, Huw ap Richard ap Sion ap Madog of Bowrda, a bard and patron of bards, was buried on Bardsey. Bodfel Hall, Llannor, which he greatly extended, is a 2* listed building.

## WILLIAM VAUGHAN, VALENTINE, BAUGH fl. 1582

Using at least three names, he operated from Wales and Studland Bay, Dorset, and in 1582 took the 300-ton German ship *Salvator* of Danzig with Stephen Heynes* (a.k.a. Carless) as consort. Heynes tortured the crew so badly to discover where they had hidden their money, that some of his own crew fell onto their knees to beg him to stop. The cargo of sugar and spices was sold openly at Studland in Dorset, and fresh cattle taken aboard. Like John Callice, Heynes had 'friends in high places' among the rich aldermen and traders of London, and was friendly with Sir Christopher Hatton, the Vice-Admiral

*Bodfel Hall, Llannor was the home of John Wyn ap Huw*

of Dorset. Heynes forced the German captain to borrow his ransom money from Francis Howley, and only released the *Salvator* to its owners upon the payment of a bribe. Heynes and Vaughan next took an English ship moored at Sandown, and its corrupt captain kept part of the cargo.

In 1583 Vaughan captured a ship loaded with Bibles, which he presented to priests and a deputy Vice-Admiral of Dorset, Francis Hawley. Hawley was noted for accepting stolen goods, and was later accused of asking pirate captains who

*The two havens on Enlli (Bardsey) from Mynydd Enlli*

moored off Studland Bay for protection money. He was offended when the pirate Clinton Atkinson (hanged 1583) did not give him an expensive looted tapestry which he had promised. Hawley then asked another pirate to catch Atkinson for him, but Captain Thomas Walton refused. Walton, like Vaughan, sailed from Dorset and Wales, and in 1581 Vaughan had fired at him to keep him away from Studland Bay. Walton later sailed with another Welsh pirate, Captain Ellis. William Vaughan was captured late in 1583, tortured to discover his accomplices, and hanged.

*Heynes in 1581 took the *Esperance* of Dieppe, which had been laden in Brazil with '*405 tons of Brazil wood, 12 puncheons of pepper, 6000 weight of cotton wool, 360 parrots, 54 munkeys, apes and other beasts.*' In June he was offering the monkeys for sale in Torbay.

## THOMAS BEAVIN
## (BETHEWIN, BEVAN) d. 1583
Originally a shoemaker, he sailed from Welsh ports and Studland Bay. After a successful career between 1580 and 1583, he was captured by royal ships, and hanged in London.

## SIR RICHARD BULKELEY 1533-1621
He was appointed Constable of Beaumaris Castle in 1561, elected the first Mayor of Beaumaris in 1562, MP for Anglesey in 1563 (and 1604 and 1614) and High Sheriff of Anglesey in 1570. He was knighted in 1577, and as Vice-Admiral of North Wales controlled Anglesey and much of Caernarfonshire. The other major landowner in Caernarfon was the Earl of Leicester, and one of his land agents, Owen Wood, of the Woods of Rhosmor, complained that Bulkeley had set up his brothers Charles and David as pirates. Wood was annoyed that Richard Bulkeley had 'tweaked' his nose in a Quarter Sessions. Wood brought his action to the Court of Star Chamber, claiming that Bulkeley had allowed Beaumaris to become a base for pirates such as Captain Purser, and had entertained the French pirate, Captain Henricke. Wood also accused Bulkeley of oppressing the townspeople of Beaumaris, and of being involved with the 1586 Babington plot. Bulkeley was exonerated by the Privy Council on these charges, but was

*Beaumaris castle*

censured in the Star Chamber for molesting Wood.

Later, it was claimed that Sir Richard was present when Henricke was captured, but *'the said Sir Richard commanded his officers not to stay him… for he said he came to land at his request… whereupon the officer did let this pyrate go for they durst do no other.'* In 1591, Richard Bulkeley received only a mild censure, as he was a leading courtier and a friend of Queen Elizabeth.

It is said that on 1 May 1602, Elizabeth I picnicked with Sir Richard Bulkeley in the Lewisham area by an oak tree, henceforward known as Honor Oak. Bulkeley's brother-in-law, Griffith John Griffith, financed his son's piracy from Beaumaris, and his son was said to have buried treasure nearby. Griffiths' ship was impounded by the Admiralty, and Richard Bulkeley bought it for a minimal amount. Sir Richard Leveson was Bulkeley's

successor as Vice-Admiral, and also allowed piracy to flourish.

## CAPTAIN WILLIAM MIDLETON (MYDDELTON), 'GWILYM CANOLDREF' c. 1550-c. 1600/1621 – *poet, soldier, sailor and translator of the Psalms*

The son of Ffowc Midleton of Archwedlog, Llansannan, Denbighshire, he was a poet, soldier and sailor, who may have been educated at Oxford. His uncle was Richard Myddelton. He was educated by William Salesbury of Llansannor, the translator of the New Testament in Welsh (see *100 Great Welshmen*). Midleton originally served under Henry Herbert, Earl of Pembroke, and composed and sang an elegy on the death of Catherine, Countess of Pembroke, in 1575. Catherine was Sir Philip Sidney's sister. In 1585-86, he was fighting with Leicester in the Netherlands, and was probably at Zutphen when Sir Philip Sidney perished. In 1589, William was in Portugal, fighting for Don Antonio's right to the throne. Also in 1589 he took a Portuguese ship out of Brazil, with a cargo of sugar, cotton wool and logwoods worth £2,700. Lord Burghley seems to refer to him as a privateer returning with a cargo of pepper from a Portuguese ship in 1590.

In that year he is known to have taken two Portuguese ships carrying spices and gems from the East Indies, worth £25,000 (£6 million today). He had won renown as a brave sailor, and in 1591 *'has the honour of having saved the English fleet which was sent to the Azores to intercept the Spanish galleons.'* He had been sent by the Earl of Cumberland to ascertain the Spanish strength, and sailed incognito among its fleet for three days. They had ten times the number of ships of Lord Thomas Howard, who had laid an ambush off the Azores. Howard and Sir Richard Grenville were awaiting the arrival of the Spanish flota from South America. Howard managed to get most of the English fleet away in time, but Grenville waited for some men to leave shore for his boat. In the ensuing battle, Grenville's *Revenge* was destroyed. At some stage Midleton also buccaneered off the Barbary Coast, and described the casting away of the *Toby* in bad conditions: *'We committed ouselves to the Lord, and began with a doleful tune and heavy hearts to*

*Chirk castle*

sing the 12th Psalm "Help, Lord for good and Godly men". Howbeit, before we had finished four verses, the waves of the sea had stopped the breaths of most of our men.'

In 1595 with Drake and Hawkins Midleton sailed to the West Indies in an attempt to take Panama, but Drake and Hawkins died, and he escaped an attack by three Spanish galleons off Cuba. While privateering, around 1596 he tranlasted the *Psalms* into Welsh. Sion Dafydd Rhys published a *Welsh Grammar* in 1592, acknowledging his debt to Midleton's learning. Midleton (as Gwilym Canoldref, his 'literal' bardic name) published in 1593 a book '*Bardhoniaeth, neu brydydhiaeth*' on the craft of the bards, and there are extant *awdlau*, *cywyddau* and *englynion* by him. Midleton wished to teach all his countrymen the poetic art, which had

previously been confined to the professional bards. In 1603, his Welsh translation of the *Psalms* into *cynghanedd* verse was posthumously published. It appears that he had completed it on board ship while buccaneering in the West Indies in 1596. He was a Renaissance gentleman, a grammarian and poet who made a major contribution to Welsh literature in the 16th century. He claimed to be the first man, along with Tomas (Tomos) Prys (q.v.) and Captain Koet, to smoke tobacco in London, which they had seized from a ship. Tobacco leaves were twisted in the form of cigars to be smoked. Tomas Prys refers to a dispute between Midleton and Sion Llwyd of Iâl (Yale, Wrexham) over a young lady. It may be that he was the Midleton who married Mary, the daughter of Stado Bruxell of Brussels, and died in Antwerp on March 27th, 1621, rather than around 1600.

## JOHN MYDDELTON 1563-1595?

He was another nephew of the wealthy Thomas and Hugh Myddelton. Although Hugh financed many buccaneering expeditions, it appears that John worked for other syndicates. Captaining the 50-ton *Moonshine*, he led raids on European vessels in 1586, 1590, and 1591, and was involved in the Azores Raid of 1586. In 1592 he took a ship off Spain on his way to the West Indies. Here John linked up with Benjamin Wood, another of Raleigh's captains in the Azores Raid. Wood was commanding three of Lord Thomas Howard's ships, but one had been lost in a storm. Near Cartagena, John Myddelton tried to take a Spanish frigate which had run aground, but Myddelton was captured with 12 other privateers.

Released, probably ransomed, Myddelton was again active in the Caribbean in 1594, privateering for Sir John Watts. Watts made enormous profits from sponsoring privateers such as Christopher Newport, Thomas Lane and Michael Geare, prompting the Venetian Ambassador to call him '*the greatest pirate that has ever been in this kingdom.*' Myddelton sailed in consort with the one-armed Christopher Newport around Trinidad and Guyana in 1594, and they took the town of Puerto Caballos in Honduras, without much booty to be shared. Myddelton then met up with other ships belonging to John Watts, captained by Richard Best in the 130-ton *Jewel* and William Lane. Off Havana, they took four prizes, including a caravel. However, the Spanish Governor sent two pinnaces which managed to capture Myddelton and seven others. He was taken to Spain in 1595 and never heard of again.

## DAVID MYDDELTON fl. 1596-1615

The Denbighshire Myddeltons were descended from Rhirid Flaidd, Lord of Penllyn (d.1207), but adopted the English name after the marriage of Rhirid ap Dafydd to the daughter of Sir Alexander Myddelton of Shrophire in 1393. The Myddeltons became a great family in North Wales, and Richard Myddelton, MP for Denbigh, had nine sons. Sir Thomas Myddelton (1550-1631) was the fourth son, who became an original shareholder in the East India Company, a partner in the chief buccaneering expeditions in the reign. He was also a partner in his brother Hugh's New River Enterprise, and also in the Virginia Company. He was MP for Merioneth, bought Chirk Castle in 1595 with his buccaneering profits and from money-lending to shippers, was knighted in 1603 and became Lord Mayor of London in 1613. Hugh Myddelton of Ruthin used the profits from his gold-smithing in the New River Project to bring fresh water to London.

The nephew of Thomas and Hugh was David Myddelton. David was the youngest of four brothers, all of whom sailed in the initial voyages of the East India Company. He was the younger brother of John and Sir Henry Myddelton. His father and all three uncles were heavily involved in the founding of the East India Company, and David jointly commanded a voyage to the West Indies in May 1601.

His captain, Sir Michael Geare, had been a privateer since at least 1588, preying on Spanish shipping. In 1596, Myddelton shared command of the *Neptune* and its pinnace with the great pirate Christopher Newport. Newport then gave the pinnace *James* to Myddelton to command, as it was far better for shallow waters than his new ship *Archangel*. In their 1601 raid they took three prizes near Cuba, bringing two back to England but losing contact with the third at sea. Geare then sailed off with Christopher Newport again, and David Myddelton joined the East India Company's Second Expedition (1604-

1606). He was second captain of *Malice Scourge*, which he renamed the *Red Dragon*, after the Welsh flag, and sailed to the East Indies with his brother Henry. David conducted negotiations with the native kings of Ternate and Tidore. He commanded the *Consent* on the Third Expedition (1607-1608). The *Consent* lost sight of her consorts in the Channel, and he sailed for the Moluccas (Spice Islands).

By secret trading Myddelton obtained a full cargo of cloves.

His irregular voyage had been incredibly profitable, and he was sent out again on the fifth voyage in a larger ship, the *Expedition*, in which he left in April 1609. At Ceram, after many difficulties, he obtained a full cargo of nutmegs and mace. On his way home he foiled an attempt of

*Penrhyn castle and Porth Penrhyn*

the Dutch to intercept him and arrived in England in the early summer of 1611.

In May 1614 he sailed once more for the East Indies in the *Samaritan*, with the *Thomas* and *Thomasine* under his orders, and arrived at Bantam on 14 February 1615. A full cargo was collected, and after sending the smaller vessels to other ports, Middleton, in the *Samaritan*, sailed for England in April 1615. His ship was wrecked on the coast of Madagascar, but the first report of Middleton's death only reached the East Indian Company on 5 September 1617. The demolished Myddelton Hall at Llanarthney near Llandeilo, now the site of the National Botanic Garden of Wales, was originally the property of David, brother of Sir Hugh Myddelton, before William Paxton bought and remodelled it.

## PIRS (PERYS, PIERS, PYRS) GRIFFITH (GRUFFUDD) 1568-1628

The son of Sir Rhys Griffith of Penrhyn Mawr near Bangor, upon his father's death in 1580 he was made a ward of court. In 1583, he was with Captain Koet and Tomas Prys when they took a prize off the coast of Africa. In 1588 he bought and provisioned a ship, and sailed from Beaumaris on April 20th, 1588. On his arrival at Plymouth on May 4th, he was honourably received by Sir Francis Drake. After fighting the Armada, Griffith joined Drake and Raleigh in expeditions against the Spanish in the West Indies. Pirs took the Spanish ship *Speranza* with its cargo of oil, olives and silk, landing at Aber Cegin in 1600. Pirs was arrested at Cork for piracy in 1603, and had to mortgage some of his estates to pay the heavy fines. It seems that he now liased with Tomas Prys* (q.v.) of Plas Iolyn in privateering, and that further heavy financial penalties led to him losing some of his estates in 1614. By 1616 he was in the Fleet prison, and his lands had been taken by mortgagers such as the Myddeltons. He had married Margaret, the daughter of Sir Thomas Mostyn, and was buried in Westminster Abbey.

*Tomas Prys was his best friend and kinsman, and wrote an ode *The Sending of the Porpoise to Prys Gruffydd to Turn Him from the Seas*, recounting that the privateer '*on the deck of his ship, very doughty in his shining armour*' (*Ar ei llong yn wrol iawn, Galw arno gloew ei harnais*) had been away from home for years:

*'Six years! Ah, how wearily they have dragged*
*Since his ship cleared the bar and bore away*
*for the High Seas'.*
*(Chwe blynedd och ai blined*
*Ar llong er pan aeth ar lled*
*I foroedd uwch y forryd*
*Dros y bar ar draws y byd.'*

Prys asked:
*'May God grant him the chiefest treasure,*
*Grace to abandon the sea! ...*
*For, after all, sea-faring is only fit for wastrels,*
*Who own not a foot of land ashore!'*

### TOMOS (THOMAS) PRYS (PRICE) 1564?-22 August 1634

His father was Elys Prys, '*The Red Doctor*' of Plas Iolyn, the grandson of Rhys ap Meredydd (Rhys Fawr) who fought with Henry Tudor at Bosworth Field. Dr Elys Prys was one of the '*three adjudicators of Caerwys*'. On his father's death in 1594, Thomas took the manor of Ysbyty Ifan and his father's clerical livings. From 1585-87 he served under Leicester in the Netherlands war. In 1599, Thomas became Sheriff of Denbighshire, then served with his mentor Robert Dudley, Earl of Leicester, in the Dutch Wars. (Sir Roger Williams, Sir Gelli Meyrick and Sir Thomas Morgan all were noted warriors in the Low Countries). He sailed under both Drake and Raleigh.In 1588, he was alongside Leicester in the army awaiting the Spanish Armada, and was present when Elizabeth I (see 100 *Great Welsh Women*) made her great speech at Tilbury.

Prys fought in France, the Netherlands, Scotland, Spain and Ireland, and became an accomplished buccaneer. At the end of the 16th century he bought a ship, fitted it out for privateering and began raiding along the coast of Spain. One of his many '*cywyddau*' reads in English '*For no mean period, I followed the seaways to Spain, across*

*Plas Iolyn, Pentrefoelas*

*the world; I believed I had only to go to sea to come by all kinds of treasure.'* He seemed happiest in later life as a pirate, living in his remote hide-out on Ynys Enlli (Bardsey island), or in the company of poet friends at Llanrwst, near his estate of Ysbyty Ifan. In the Llanrwst taverns, he describes the times when his fellow 'lions' used to roar under the effects of drink... *'When the beer begins to flow, then is pandemonium let loose in Llanrwst.'* Of his friend David Salisbury of Llanrhaiadr, he said, *'no Christian man was more famed for his prowess in a fight'*, and of the ex-soldier Gawain Goodman *'if he once gets at all the wines of a town, he'll not come home without tripping: well I know how he can drink his share; if there's sack to be had, he'll not put up with gruel. A generous and a godly man is Gawain – when in his cups! But not so much as a pin will you get out of him till the pot has warmed his head.'* Thomas Owen was *'that fierce, fiery-handed man of war'*, and his great friends Pyrs Gruffudd (Griffith, q.v.) and William Midleton (q.v.) are also mentioned, the latter in relation to an impending deul because of a love affair.

A landowner, Thomas Prys was one of the first three men to smoke tobacco publicly in London, with his friend William Myddelton (q.v.) and Captain Koet (Coet). It was ransacked from a ship which the three captains took between the Canary Islands and Africa. Prys came to know London well, not only its great houses, but also its taverns and brothels, but tired of living there, and came to hate that city. In a cywydd he explained to his son that London was Hell, and warned him against all officialdom. He had been in London as a soldier of Elizabeth, but left there to return to Wales. Thomas used his freedom as a nobleman to 'bring a breath of fresh sea air into the stalling *cywdd*'. His poem *'Cywydd y ddangos yr hildring a fu i wr pan oedd ar y mor'* is a humorous

*Ysbyty Ifan*

account of his privateering expedition, and one translated couplet reads '*Before I will, pill or part, Buy a ship, I'll be a shephart*'. He also devoted some poems on his buccaneering to Pyrs Griffith (q.v.), who was carrying out the same activities. He organised his activities from Bardsey island (see John Wyn ap Hugh), but resided at Plas Iolyn. Apart from frequenting the taverns of Llanrwst, he spent a great deal of time in London, using up his money in '*litigation and dissipation*'. There is a vivid description of contemporary London in his collection of poetry '*Cywydd i ddangos mai Uffern yw Llundain.*' Many of his poems are still extant, including many dedicated to *Eiddig* (the jealous one). Two of his poems are entitled '*Ode to show that London is Hell*' and '*Ode to show how a young man was cheated out of his money through drabbing and dicing when he first went to London.*' Tomos describes a bawdy London of brothels and taverns, where '*life is short and precarious, the home of all the knavery and bawdery in the world...*' and he is '*carousing with a drab at a tavern as boldly as you please.*' The Welsh poem goes on about his '*going thence to the shady quarter, bent upon gaming ('twas an easy job to knock up against congenial comanions in the city). Then to the dice-tables, warming to the game and calling a "sixer" on a poor cast... Detecting the wiles of "doctored" dice and swearing like a madman; perjuring oneself stoutly when found out; storming and blustering in no sweet terms, and brawling with naked weapons.*' In one of his poems he sends a porpoise to carry a message to his cousin Pyrs Gruffudd (q.v.) to give up piracy before it was too late. To some extent his rejuvenation of the *cywydd* verse form, with an injection of freshness and humour, enabled it to survive as the most frequently used and enjoyed of all the older Welsh verse forms in Welsh, in the present day. Over 200 of his poems survive, many recounting his experiences in the French Wars of Religion and facing the Armada. He is buried in Ysbyty Ifan churchyard.

## WILLIAM HUGHES (HUGHS) fl. 1611

Richard Bishop of Yarmouth was a privateer from 1591, who sailed in consort with John Ward to Tunis in 1605. The Atlantic pirates elected Bishop the 'admiral' of their confederation in 1608, with Captain Peter Easton as vice-admiral. In 1609, they commanded 9 ships and 1,000 men based in Ireland, and with impunity, the fleet plundered English and Dutch shipping in the Bristol Channel. In 1610, Captain Parker sold a three-quarter share of his confederation ship to

*Elizabethan smokers in a public house*

Thomas Hussey, who now commanded the *Black Raven*, a captured 160-tom Flemish fly-boat with 23 guns. William Hughes was another of the pirate captains, and as they were all summoned around Hussey's deathbed in 1611. Hussey gave the *Black Raven* and all his loot to Hughes. Bishop retired in 1611, and Easton became the pirates' admiral, leading a fleet of up to 17 ships. James I was reduced to offering the pirates a pardon, and allowed Dutch men-of-war to patrol British coastal waters in the hope that they would curb the pirates. However, Easton led his fleet in searching for their would-be destroyers, and took two of the Dutch fleet.

In August 1611, the confederacy broke up, and Hughes now sailed with Peter Easton and a Captain Harvey to West Africa, taking Dutch and English ships. Easton told a captured captain that he believed that Englishmen were no better than '*Turckes and Jews*'. The three captains then headed for Newfoundland, seeking more ships and bigger crews. They 'forced' around 500 Britons and another six ships to join their flotilla, but several hundred men deserted in one Newfoundland raid, mainly because of Easton's unpredictable nature and cruelty. Easton returned to Salé (modern Rabat in Morocco) in 1612, and negotiated a pardon from the Duke of Savoy, Carlo Emanuele I. He retired under his protection to Villefranche, built a palace and married an heiress. Hughes' fate is unknown.

## JOHN NORMAN fl. 1631

This pirate sailed into Pwllheli harbour in February 1631 and took a Scottish barque. Deputy Vice-Admiral Gruffydd Madryn, a cousin of John Griffiths, was unable to arrest him because of a lack of support. Norman repaired his ship at anchor, and the townspeople informed him that the Vice Admiral John Griffiths was on his way, so that he could escape. Captain Henry Mainwaring (q.v.) called Wales '*the nursery and store-house of pirates*' because of its natural hidden harbours and the ease with which they could escape to open seas.

## ADMIRAL SIR THOMAS BUTTON c.1575-April 1634

More of a naval man and an explorer, nevertheless he took part in some privateering adventures. He was the fourth son of Miles Button, Sheriff of Glamorgan (1565, 1571 and 1589) and of Margaret Lewis of The Van, Caerphilly. He was born at Worlton near the site of the present Dyffryn House and its fabulous gardens, near St Lythans in the Vale of Glamorgan. He first went to sea in 1589, and then again in 1592 was at sea, seemingly sailing under Drake, Hawkins and Raleigh. By 1601, when the Spanish fleet invaded Ireland, he had become captain of the pinnace *Moon*, and acquitted himself with such distinction as to win commendation and a lifetime pension of six shillings eight pence. The following year he commanded a privateer, the *Wylloby*, in the West Indies. With rapid promotion, in 1604 Button was given a pension for distinguished service in the West Indies and in Ireland by the Lord High Admiral. In 1609 he commanded a ship, and in 1610 was a member of the company known as the 'Incorporated Discoverers' of the North-West Passage. It was formed under the patronage of Prince Henry, to find a passage from the Atlantic to the Pacific around the north coast of America.

In 1612 Button was made a member of the North West Company and given the command of an expedition of two ships, the *Resolution* and the *Discovery*, to North America to try to find and rescue Henry Hudson, whom mutineers had put adrift in a small boat. Button was also to carry on further exploration of the Northwest Passage. The expedition entered Hudson Strait, where he named Resolution Island after his own vessel. He found no trace of Hudson but sailed through the strait and southwest across Hudson Bay to Nelson River, where he was iced in over a brutal winter. Many men died, including Button's sailing master, for whom the Nelson River is named. The crew lived off ptarmigan which were plentiful in the area.

He named the mainland New Wales, and also named Button's Bay and Mansell's Islands. In the spring and through the summer of 1613 Button and his crew continued their explorations, finally sailing for home in August. At 60 degrees latitude he found a current flowing in from the west, which he believed to be the key to the North-West Passage, and called it Hubbart's Hope. However, his instructions forbade him to follow it, and he reluctantly returned home, to be knighted by James I. A year later his neighbour and cousin Captain Gibbon was sent out to explore the current, his mate being a man named Baffin, after whom Baffin's Bay was named. Button was knighted in 1616. He did not return to Canada, although he remained in service.

Button was then appointed Admiral of the Irish Seas, a position he held for most of the remainder of his life, except for the period of the Algerine Expedition of 1620-21, under the command of Sir Robert Mansell (the Welsh uncle after whom he had named Mansell's Islands). Button was Rear-Admiral, and complained to Mansell that he should have been Vice-Admiral instead of Sir Richard Hawkins. Mansell placated him by saying that he had not known at the time that Button was leaving his Irish post to join the venture. For most of the rest of his life, Button was chasing Barbary corsairs, and Dunkirk and Biscay pirates off the west coast of Ireland in the *Antelope*, then in the *Phoenix*, and finally in the *Lion*. The Lion had '*twelve whelps*', a squadron with many of his kinsmen as commanders, and sailed the seas from Kinsale to the Scilly Isles, from Dublin to Lundy and Bristol and St George's Channels.

Button had to mortgage his own estates around Cardiff to fit out these privateers, and he wrote in 1629 from Cardiff that he was '*kept back, not in so good a case as I was ten years ago, for then I owed nothing, but now for five years past receiving neither pension nor pay ... but in my house debarred from my wonted freedom by reason I have no means to pay what I owe (than which affliction of this latter not to be able to pay every man his own this world cannot lay a greater on me)...'* He feared that he and his family would have *'either to beg or starve.'* The Navy Board complained that he listened to no-one but Buckingham, but Mansell and the Earl of Denbigh always came to the defence of *'old Tom Button'*. He took several prizes, which involved him in law-suits and also enabled him to defend himself and pay of some debts. He was in command of the *Convertive* and spotted four French ships chasing a small Welsh ship. He captured one, laden with salt and cognac, and intended to take it to Bristol. Prevailing winds meant that he landed it in Milford, and he spent many years in litigation as to the extent of his prize money. He was constantly asking for better guns for his 'whelps' in fighting the 'Turks' (the Barbary corsairs taking slaves from coastal villages). In 1625, three 'Turkish' pirate ships took all the inhabitants off Lundy into slavery, and also kidnapped several people from Padstow and threatened to burn Ilfracombe.

Button's independent mind and outspoken criticism of the Navy Board led to a reputation for insubordination and a series of legal disputes with the Admiralty. These legal disputes, in addition to his previous debts, impoverished him and remained unresolved at his death. Despite his standing in the Navy, his career was marked by prolonged quarrels with the Admiralty, resulting in the end with him in ill-health, being stripped of his post as Admiral and left effectively bankrupt. He was buried on 8 April 1634 at the church of St Margaret's, Westminster, survived by his wife and five of their seven children. He left no will and his Welsh lands passed to his eldest son, Miles, who had to mortgage them to meet his father's debts. After waiting three years, his widow received £650 (about £94,000 pounds today) from the government in settlement of pay and expenses he was owed.

Button married Mary, daughter of Sir Walter Rice of Dynevor. Their son Miles married Barbara, the heiress of Rhys Meurig of Cottrell Manor (the present golf course in the Vale), and their daughter

Elizabeth married Colonel John Poyer, who was executed by Cromwell at Covent Garden for defending Pembroke Castle with the Royalists. Sir Thomas Button himself was said to be a relative of Oliver Cromwell, whose real name was Williams. His burial place is unrecorded.

## DAVID JONES – '*Davy* (*Davey*) *Jones's Locker*' fl. 1636

In 1634, Charles I was bribed by some London merchants to give a secret privateering commission to capture ships below the Equator, from countries which did not have a peace treaty with England. One covert commission was given to Richard Oldfield of the *Samaritan* and to William Cobb of the *Roebuck*, to 'range and discover' the African coast. Another secret commission was a licence to plunder '*especially from the Cape to China and Japan, including the Red Sea, Persian Gulf and Coromandel Coast.*' The last three areas broke the monopoly of the East India Company. When the seals were broken, off Cape Verde, Captain Oldfield asked to be put ashore as the expedition was plainly illegal.

David Jones was made sailing-master,

and in effect was the real authority on board both ships. The two ships became separated, and the *Samaritan* foundered in the Comoros Islands off Madagascar. Captain Cobb began building a new sloop at Mohilla. The *Roebuck*, under Captain William Ayres, then took an Arabian junk in the Gulf of Aden. On September 5th, Ayres and Jones attacked the Indian ship *Taufiqi* in the Red Sea, although it had a sailing pass issued by the East India Company. Ayres seems to have led the crew in torturing the passengers and crew.

Jones was now in charge of a lightly manned, recently taken prize ship, filled with loot, accompanying Ayres in the *Roebuck*. The outrage led to the East India Company commissioning two ships to seek out Ayres, Cobb and Jones. The East India Company ship *Swan* under Captain John Proud took Ayres' ship, with Cobb now on board, in 1636 off the Comoros Islands. Jones knew he could not escape with his own heavily laden ship, so he scuttled it with all its incriminating evidence – the booty was put into '*Davy Jones' Locker*', i.e. the seabed. The East India Company captain fined the privateers £10,000 in booty, but allowed them to keep the *Roebuck*. Two more Indian ships were taken in 1636, and the ship returned to England with £40,000 in loot in May 1637. Most of the booty was claimed by Charles I and the promoters, leaving about £10,000 to be shared between the officers and 50 crew. Cobb and Ayres were arrested and briefly imprisoned in 1643. Jones disappeared from history.

The first clear reference to Davy Jones's Locker is in Tobias Smollet's *The Adventures of Peregrine Pickle in 1751*: '*By the*

*Dinefwr castle and estate*

*Lord, Jack, you may say what you will; but I'll be damned if it was not Davey Jones himself. I know him by his saucer eyes, his three rows of teeth, and tail, and the blue smoke that came out of his nostrils. This same Davy Jones, according to the mythology of sailors, is the fiend that presides over all the evil spirits of the deep, and is often seen in various shapes, perching among the rigging on the eve of hurricanes, ship-wrecks, and other disasters to which sea-faring life is exposed, warning the devoted wretch of death and woe.*' Davy Jones was a spirit, or sea-devil who lived on the ocean floor. Sending someone to '*Davy Jones's locker*' meant despatching them to the ocean's depths. The '*locker*' was the bottom of the sea, the last resting place for sunken ships and bones. '*Old Davy*' was also known as the devil from the 18th century. Another source tells us that David Jones ran a London tavern, with his own press gang and drugged his unwary patrons, storing them in the ale lockers at the back of the inn until they could be taken aboard some departing ship. Phrases from these times include the following: '*I'll see you in Davy Jones's*' (a threat to kill someone); '*He's in Davy's grip*' (he is scared, or close to death); and '*he has the*

*Davys*' or '*he has the Joneseys*' (he is frightened).

## NICHOLAS HOOKES (HAWKES) '*the great pyrate*' d. 1637

In St Mary's Church, Conwy, there is a 17th century marble slab in the chancel inscribed to Nicholas Hookes, and stating that he was the father of 27 children and himself a 41st child: '*Here lieth the body of Nicholas Hookes, of Conway, gentleman, who was one-and-fortieth child of his father, William Hookes, Esq., by Alice, his wife, and the father of 27 children. He died 20th of March, 1637.*' Lewis Dwnn, in his *Visitations of Wales* notes '*the great pyrate*', the 15th son of a merchant in Conwy, who practised piracy and smuggling from bases at St Tudwal's isle and Enlli (Bardsey island). The author would welcome more information upon this intriguing and mysterious character.

## ADMIRAL SIR ROBERT MANSELL 1573-1653

Born at Margam in Glamorgan, he first went to sea with Lord Howard, and probably faced the Armada. He served with Sir Christopher Blunt's regiment when Howard and Essex sacked Cadiz in 1596, for which he was knighted. In 1596, Mansell was the captain of Essex's own ship in the 'Islands Voyage' of Essex and Raleigh. From 1599, he was in charge of a small squadron operating off the Irish coast, reinforced in 1600 by Sir Richard Leveson. In that year, he fought a rapier duel with Sir John Heydon in Norfolk, and was reported killed, but after Essex's rebellion was engaged in arresting the Earl's accomplices. Given a squadron to guard the coast, he joined with Sir Amyas Preston (of the Preston and Somers 1595 Expedition fame), and they took six Portuguese '*Easterlings*' laden with booty.

In September 1602, Mansell intercepted six Spanish galleys, heading towards Flanders. He had waited for them off Dungeness, while his Dutch consorts patrolled Dunkirk and the Downs. The galleys fell into the trap. Two were rammed, two wrecked in a gale, and two taken by the Dutch. For this exploit, he was created Vice-Admiral of the Fleet, and Admiral of the Narrow Seas. Commanding Dutch and English ships, his fleet took more prizes, including a Portuguese carrack with a cargo of pepper in 1603. '*The proud Welshman*' was given the honour of escorting the Spanish and French ambassadors from Calais to England on their 1603 peace mission, and prevented Admiral de Rosny from flying the French flag. In that year, he also escorted Sir Walter Raleigh from Winchester to his London trial. He was made Treasurer of the Navy in 1604 and Vice-Admiral of the Realm in 1618, and in 1620 led the Algerine Expedition in his flagship *Lion*. There were six men-of-war and thirteen armed merchant ships, but the engagement was inconclusive. The Barbary States centred on Algiers had a fleet of thirty ships and ten galleys.

A keen politician and speaker, he had been imprisoned briefly in the Marshalsea in 1613 for political disaffection. Mansell was MP for Kings Lynn in 1601 (the year after his nearby duel), for Carmarthen in 1603, Carmarthenshire in 1614, Glamorgan in 1623 and 1625, Lostwithiel in 1626, and again for Glamorgan 1627-28. He had a strong interest in glass manufacture, as shown when the application for a monopoly for the new process, of making glass from coal instead of wood, was granted in 1615. King James expressed his

*Ynysoedd Tudwal, St Tudwal's islands, were commonly used by Welsh smugglers such as Nicholas Hookes*

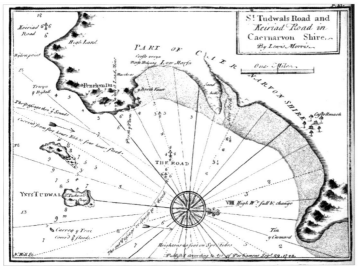

great wonderment 'that Robert Mansell, who had won so much honour on water should meddle with fire.' He built several glass-works to protect his share of the monopoly, including one on the Tyne to make use of the abundant sea-coal in the region. His first marriage was to the daughter of the Lord Keeper, and his second to one of the Queen's Maids of Honour in 1617. He was one of the canopy bearers at the Queen's funeral in 1619.

*The gravestone in Conwy church*

## HENRY MAINWARING 1587-1653
### *The Most Famous Sea Rover of His Day*

From the Welsh borders in Shropshire, Sir Henry Mainwaring was the most famous of all the Jacobean pirates. The Mainwarings were an old Cheshire family, who had been in Shropshire and Cheshire since the early 12th century at least. The best account of his life is the two-volume account *The Life and Works of Sir Henry Mainwaring* edited by his descendant G.E. Mainwaring, and published by The Navy Records Society in 1920. The publication also includes Henry Mainwaring's *Of the Beginnings, Practices and Suppression of Pirates* and his The Seaman's Dictionary. Gosse (1932) says '*not only was he a most successful pirate himself, without equal in England*' but '*Mainwaring was one of those geniuses who lived at the wrong time. There can be little doubt that had he been born fifty years later, his fame would have equalled that of the great navigators Drake or Raleigh.*'

At the age of 15, Henry gained a degree from Brasenose College, Oxford, in 1602. After trying his hand at being a lawyer at the Inner Temple, then as a soldier in a volunteer regiment in the Low Countries, he went to sea as a privateer in 1611, aged just 24. He was given a commission by the Lord High Admiral to capture the troublesome pirate Captain Peter Easton (Eston). From 1610 the 'Pirate Admiral' Easton was in command of a fleet of 40 ships, controlling Bristol Channel shipping from the mouth of the Avon. With ten ships Easton went to Newfoundland for fresh supplies, and at Harbour Grace took five ships, a hundred cannon, goods, and enlisted 500 English cod splitters to join his force. He was the first pirate to raid the Avalon coast of Newfoundland since Sir John Perrot.

Mainwaring could not capture Easton, who took advantage of the Duke of Savoy's offer of using the free port of Villefranche. Bonded warehouses were opened for the storage of his booty, and he retired to a palace there, in which he was reckoned to have £2,000,000 worth of gold stashed away. Mainwaring turned pirate as soon as he reached the Straits of Gibraltar. From a base at Marmora (Mehedia, near Rabat) and another at Broadhaven in Ireland he attacked Atlantic shipping. In 1612 the Lord High Admiral had given Mainwaring a letter of marque to savage Spanish ships in the Caribbean. In his 120-ton *Resistance*, Mainwaring sailed to Gibraltar and informed his crew that it was not really necessary to take the scurvy-ridden trip to the West Indies in order to hit the Spaniards. Mainwaring had bought the *Resistance* from the famed shipwright Phineas Pett, and wanted to get his money back quickly. He instead proposed to head for Marmora on the Atlantic Barbary Coast and use that as his base, to attack any '*Juan-Carlos*' (Spaniard) in sight. This is the origin of the term of abuse 'wanker', as recounted in Exquemelin's *The Buccaneers of America*, dated 1684-8. We find the following description by Captain Ringrose after his being shipwrecked. Some Indians asked about six men (prisoners) in Ringrose's company who spoke a different language and kept apart from the British privateers: '*We told them they were "Wankers", which is the name they commonly give to the Spaniards in their own language. Their next question was, if they should kill those Spaniards; but I answered them: "No, by no means; I would not consent to have it done."* '

Mamora was on the mouth of the Sibu River, not far from Salé. (Salé is modern Rabat in Morocco, and was the main pirate haven on the Atlantic coast. In the 1620's Barbary corsairs from Salé raided England for slaves, and held Lundy Island for two weeks). In return for protection, the British pirates at Mamora taught Moroccans gunnery and sailing, and shared their booty with them. Not until 1614 was it captured, by a huge Spanish expedition of 99 ships and 7000 troops. Mainwaring's privateers willingly agreed, to sail to this pirate paradise, and from the summer of 1613 to the summer of 1614, around 30 ships had been taken. The King of Spain sent the Duke of Medina to offer Mainwaring a high post in his own service plus money to join him, so as to stop the depredations on Spanish shipping. Mainwaring had refused to take any English prizes, but could not return to England, having over-ridden the authority of his letters of commission. The Spanish regarded him as the reincarnation of the fiendish '*El Draque*', as '*hardly a ship passed his lair without either suffering damage or capture.*' At this time, the Duke of Florence and the Bey of Tunis respectively asked Mainwaring to privateer on their behalf, but he refused.

Like Easton, Mainwaring therefore had to go to Newfoundland to recruit amongst the disillusioned English cod-splitters and merchant seamen there. He led a fleet of eight ships, and pillaged the fishing fleets there for 4 months, in the company of Easton, his original target for capture. 1614 Records state that '*Captain Mainwaring with divers other captains arrived in Newfoundland the 4th June, having eight sails of war-like ships, one whereof they took at the bank, another upon the main of Newfoundland, from all the harbours whereof they commanded carpenters, mariners, victuals, munitions and all necessaries from the fishing fleet after this rate – of every six mariners they take one, and the one-fifth part of all their victuals: from the Portugal ships they took all their wine and other provisions, save their bread: from a French ship in Harbour Grace they took 10,000 fish; some of the company of many ships did run away unto them. They took a French ship fishing in Carbonear, and so after they had continued three months and a half taking their pleasure of the fishing fleet, the 14th September 1614, they departed, having with them from the* fishing fleet about 400 mariners and fishermen: many volunteers, many compelled.' Compulsion was not usually used, except for 'sea-artists' in the last resort. Usually, normal seamen pretended that they had been 'forced' to join 'the sweet trade', and were given letters to this effect by buccaneer and pirate captains. These letters were 'insurance policies' should they ever come to trial. Carbonear's first mention in history is due to Mainwaring's raid – it is between Harbour Grace and Victoria on the Avalon Peninsula.

Mainwaring returned to Marmora, but found that the Spanish had taken his base in his absence. He did not bother trying to storm its defences, as he knew that Easton had retired to the safe port of Villefranche, under the protection of the Duke of Savoy, Carlos Emmanuele I. There Mainwaring linked up with another exiled pirate captain called Walsingham. Within six weeks, he had taken loot off the Spanish valued at 500,000 Spanish crowns, and brought its Mediterranean shipping to a virtual standstill. The King of Spain despatched five warships, expressly to bring him back dead or alive. Off Cadiz, Mainwaring's three ships decisively beat the Spanish flotilla, however, which was forced to flee to Lisbon. The King now promised Mainwaring a free pardon and 20,000 ducats a year to lead a fleet of Spanish ships, but he again refused. The Bey of Tunis again offered a similar deal if Mainwaring would take the Islamic faith and lead the Barbary corsairs.

King James, with Catholic sympathies, was constantly being asked by the French and Spanish ambassadors to stop Henry Mainwaring's depredations on their shipping, so he sent an envoy to Mainwaring. The privateer was offered a free pardon to give up piracy, with the (somewhat empty) threat that an English fleet would be sent to capture him if he refused. Mainwaring returned to Dover in 1616 and he and his crews were pardoned, and allowed to keep their booty.

Sir Henry now found a new role in capturing pirates, chasing the Barbary Corsairs away from the British coast, and was knighted in 1618. In the same year he became a Gentleman of the King's Bedchamber. In 1620 Mainwaring was appointed Lieutenant of Dover Castle and Deputy Warden of the Cinque Ports and a year later was elected an MP, ending his career as a Vice-Admiral. From 1618, he was not only a respected courtier, but a friend of the King and Prince Charles. As a naval commissioner, he held command in several expeditions, and wrote more books, including *The Seaman's Dictionary* in 1644, which for a century was the standard text for naval terms. Mainwaring, who rose from a common pirate to knighthood and Admiral in the navy, summed up the expediency of his times: *'The State may hereafter want such men who are commonly the most serviceable in war.'*

## ADMIRAL SIR HENRY MORGAN 1635-1688
### *'The Greatest of All the Brethren of the Coast'*, *'The Sword of England'*, The Greatest Privateer of All Time

Henry Morgan was born a younger son at Llanrhymni Hall, a mansion and estate to the east of Cardiff, and his father's brothers were opposing colonels in the English Civil War. Morgan served in Cromwell's *'Western Design'* to take Hispaniola in 1654, and when the Penn-Venables unsuccessful expedition instead took Jamaica, he stayed there to seek his fortune. His uncle Colonel Edward Morgan was Lieutenant-Governor of Jamaica, and Henry Morgan married his daughter, Mary. By 1661 Commodore Christopher Myngs had appointed Morgan captain of his first vessel, and Morgan sailed under Myngs in 1663, destroying Santiago de Cuba. Morgan next sailed with John Morris and Captain Jackman in 1665 and they sacked Spanish settlements at Vildemos (on the Tabasco River in the Bay of Campeche, Mexico), Trujillo in Honduras and Granada in Mexico.

Lord Windsor, the new Governor of Jamaica, refused to stop his privateers from attacking Spanish ships, believing, like Morgan, that attack was the best form of defence. The pro-Spanish Charles II therefore replaced Windsor with Sir Thomas Modyford, but Modyford again agreed with his friend Morgan, that the only survival strategy for the English colony to survive, was by weakening the Spanish possessions and shipping that surrounded them. When Morgan returned to Jamaica, Modyford had received letters from Charles II to stop 'piracy' but continued to issue letters of marque to attack Spanish and Dutch shipping.

Modyford now commissioned Edward

Mansvelt to assemble 15 ships and 500-600 men to attack the Dutch settlement of Curaçao. Morgan had captured several ships off the Mexican coast of Campeche, and was appointed vice-admiral. However, at sea most captains decided that Curaçao was not lucrative enough for the risks involved. Many privateers now deserted the expedition, but Mansvelt and Morgan decided to attack Santa Catalina and Providence Island. The Spanish were unprepared and surrendered all of their forts, and all but one was destroyed. Privateers stayed on the island to gather its wealth, while Morgan and Mansvelt sailed back to Jamaica to gather reinforcements. Modyford appointed his brother, Sir James, as Governor of Providence. Mansfield was captured and killed by the Spanish shortly afterwards, and the privateers elected the impressive Morgan as their new 'Admiral of the Brethren of the Coast'.

With no income except for privateering, it seems that Morgan told Modyford that the Spanish were going to attack and capture Jamaica, and his ever-willing friend provided yet another commission, asking Morgan to capture Spaniards in Cuba to interrogate them about the forthcoming 'invasion'. Modyford and Charles II, and the king's brother James as Lord of the Admiralty, took a cut of the profits of any privateering expeditions. However, Morgan had a clause written into his letters of marque that their share would only come from ships taken at sea, not from overland targets, so his men had a third more loot to share between them.

Morgan assembled 10 ships by sailing to pirate havens and granting commissions, gathering 500 men. He wished to take Havana, but it was too heavily defended, and in 1667 Morgan landed on Cuba to take Puerto Principe. However, a Spanish prisoner that Morgan held hostage escaped, and warned the citizens who quickly deserted the town with their valuables. After searching, only 58,000 pieces of eight were taken, not enough to pay off his Jamaican debts, so Morgan decided to raid the third most important Spanish city in the New World, Porto Bello, well protected by three great Spanish forts. With information from a prisoner, the forts were taken and the city entered. The Spanish counterattacked, but

Morgan organized an ambush of the more powerful Spanish fleet, in a narrow passage. After two months of sacking and ransoming, his men collected 100,000 pieces of eight and valuables worth another 100,000 pieces of eight. England had sent Modyford *HMS Oxford* to protect Port Royal, and he handed it to Morgan. Attacked by the English authorities, Modyford wrote to them that his commissions were utterly necessary to protect Jamaica, 'proving' his point by giving Morgan another letter of marque.

900 privateers of all nations, in 11 ships flocked to join the multilingual and unbeatable Morgan at the Île de Vache off Haiti. His next target Cartagena was one of Spain's most defended cities, holding all the gold and silver in transit from Peru to Spain. The captains celebrated the decision, but that night a fuse was accidentally lit on the *Oxford*, near the gunpowder stores, and the new flagship was blown to oblivion, with several captains dying. Somehow Morgan was rescued from the water and survived, and in March 1669 led 10 ships and 800 men to attack Cartagena. Storms and headwinds meant that his number of crew had

Sʳ HEN: MORGAN

*Admiral Sir Henry Morgan*

dropped to just 500 men, too weak to attack Cartagena, and Maracaibo in Venezuela was selected instead. It was at the inner end of Lake Maracaibo, a huge lake reached through a shallow channel, and protected by a great fort. The fleet could not pass the fort without being destroyed, and Morgan landed to attack it. After several attacks, strangely, it had been abandoned, but a privateer spotted a slow-burning fuse meant to blow up the powder stores, the fort and all the enemy within. Everyone ran away, but Morgan ran towards the fuse and extinguished it. Delays meant that most of the citizens of Maracaibo were able to escape with their valuables into the jungle. Morgan took what he could and set off to attack nearby Gibraltar. After collecting booty and ransoming Gibraltar's residents, Morgan loaded his ships to return to Jamaica. However, the fort had been retaken by the Spanish, and guarding the narrow entrance from Lake Maracaibo to the open ocean were stationed the Spanish men-of-war *Magdalena*, *Santa Luisa* and *Nuestra Señora de Soledad*.

Sending a fireship, Morgan destroyed the Magdalena, and captured the *Nuestra Señora de Soledad*, while the Santa Luisa was run ashore. Morgan was still unable to cross the channel because of the fort's cannon, but he spent the day in sight of the fort, shifting men in rowboats to the forests onshore. However, they all returned to their ships, hidden on the floor of the boats. The Spanish expected a night attack from inland by all the men who had

*The town of Puerto del Principe taken and sacked by Henry Morgan in 1667*

'landed', and moved all their cannon from covering the sea passage, to the inland side of the fort. That night, Morgan used the tide to drift all his ships through the passage, unnoticed. Morgan returned to Port Royal on 27 May 1669 in his new flagship, *Nuestra Señora de Soledad*. Returning to Jamaica, he was officially reproved, but not punished by Modyford, who instead made him commander-in-chief of all the ships of war in Jamaica.

Panama, on the Pacific coast, the richest city in New Spain, had never been taken, and Morgan gathered men to march across the Isthmus, and sack it. Morgan recaptured the island of Santa Catalina from Spain on 5 December 1670, and on 27 December took the fortress of San Lorenzo, Panama, killing 300 men of the garrison and leaving just 23 alive. Morgan left 200 men to guard his ships, and with 1,200 men he advanced through jungle towards the Pacific coast and Panama City. Constantly being ambushed, and suffering sickness, thirst and starvation, by 28 January 1671, the privateers met the Spanish in battle on the plains outside the city. Morgan won the pitched battle against superior forces, and a new city of Panama had to be built after it was set on fire (by the Spanish, not Morgan). The sack of Panama violated a peace treaty, and Morgan was arrested and taken to London in 1672. However, Charles II could not punish his country's greatest hero, known as 'the Sword of England', as his régime was still unstable. His reign had already seen the Great Plague, the Great Fire of London and the Dutch destroying the royal fleet in

*The capture of Puerto Bello, showing Morgan taking Fort Triana 1668*

the Medway, sailing off with his new flagship. Instead of any punishment, Morgan was feted across London and knighted in 1674, before returning to Jamaica in 1675 as Lieutenant-Governor.

An account of Morgan's exploits was published by Alexandre Exquemelin, once his confidante, in a Dutch volume entitled *De Americaensche Zee-Roovers* (*History of the Buccaneers of America*). Morgan successfully

*The Spanish Armada destroyed by Captain Morgan on Lake Maracaibo Venezuela in 1669*

was buried in Palisadoes cemetery, Port Royal, which sank beneath the sea after the 1692 earthquake. As with 'Black Bart' Roberts, it is impossible to do justice to his remarkable career, and this author has written his biography, *Admiral Sir Henry Morgan – the Greatest Buccaneer of Them All*.

brought the first libel suit in history against the book's publishers, securing a retraction and damages of £200. This author has translated Exqumelin's accounts of Morgan's expeditions as *The Illustrated Pirate Diaries – A Remarkable Eye-Witness Account of Henry Morgan and the Buccaneers*. Upon Morgan's death, he was laid in state at the King's House in Port Royal, and all the ships anchored in the harbour fired broadsides in salute. He

An old West Indian ballad has the lines:
*'Ho! Harry Morgan sails today*
*Across the Spanish Main.*
*What a pretty bill for the Dons to pay*
*Ere he comes back again'*
(In the Caribbean and Central America, the Spanish owned everything except Barbados, Tortuga and Jamaica, so wherever he went, the Spanish suffered and had to rebuild)

The chorus is:
*'Him cheat him friend of him last guinea*
*Him kill both friar and priest –*
*Oh dear!*
*Him cut de t'roat of picanniny*
*Bloody, bloody buccaneer.'*
(A picanniny was a small black child –
from the Spanish *pequeño* – small).
Morgan was one of the greatest generals in history, having invaded inland Spanish possessions on six occasions, defeating greater forces each time. Arthur Glyn Prys-Jones's wonderful poem *Morgan's March to Panama* reads:

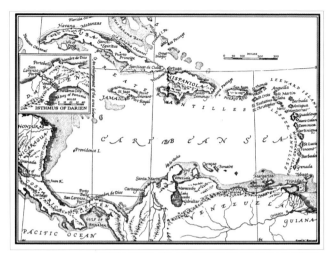

*Morgan's Area of Operations – the Caribbean and the Americas*

'Morgan's curls are matted,
His lips are cracked and dry,
His tawny beard is tangled,
And his plumed hat hangs awry:
... But his voice still booms like thunder
Through the foetid jungle glade
As he marches, bold as Lucifer,
Leading his gaunt brigade.
...Twelve hundred famished buccaneers
Blistered, bitten and bled,

A stricken mob of men accursed
By the monstrous sun o'erhead:
...Twelve hundred starveling scarecrows
Without a crumb to eat,
And not a drink for tortured throats
In that grim, festering heat.
...Twelve hundred threadbare musketeers
Rotting in tropic mud
Where the reeking, fevered mangroves
Wreak havoc in their blood:
...Twelve hundred febrile wretches,
A legion of the dead:

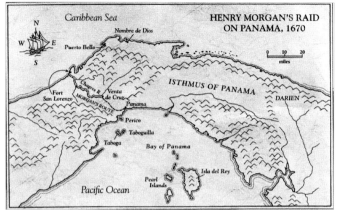

*Map showing Morgan's route to Panama*

*But Morgan in his blue brocade*
*Goes striding on ahead.*
*...Twelve hundred tatterdemalions,*
*The sorriest, maddest crew*
*That ever the green savannahs saw*
*When the Spanish bugles blew:*
*...Twelve hundred rattling skeletons*
*Who sprang to life, and then*
*Like a wild wave took Panama,*
*For they were Morgan's men.'*

## MORRIS (MAURICE) WILLIAMS
### fl. 1659-64

He was noted as having bought *La Abispa* (*The Wasp*), a captured Spanish prize, by 'inch of candle' in May 1659 at Cagway (Port Royal), Jamaica. It had been captured by the naval frigate *Diamond*, and renamed *Jamaica*. Williams then received a privateering commission from Governor Edward D'Oyley, who sold him five cannon and issued a proclamation allowing Williams to recruit sailors from the naval frigate *Marston Moor*. Upon April 21st, 1664, Colonel Edward Morgan carried Charles II's instructions to Barbados to Sir Thomas Modyford. Modyford, a successful planter, and Governor of Barbados since 1660, was to be the new Governor of Jamaica, with Edward Morgan as his deputy-governor. On June 1st Modyford landed in Jamaica, and followed the king's instructions by forbidding hostilities with Spain and ending the practice of issuing letters of marque. The privateers, including the redoubtable Captain Myngs,

Old Panama's Cathedral Tower where the Spanish sought refuge from Morgan

proceeds sent to the Spanish owner. This discouraged any other privateers from coming to Port Royal. However, it appears that Williams had previously carefully ransacked the prize before Modyford took it, as Modyford wrote in February 1665: '*The Spanish prizes have been inventoried and sold, but it is suspected that those of Morrice Williams and Bernard Nicholls have been miserably plundered, and the interested parties will find but a slender account in the Admiralty.*'

were reluctant to halt their trade, however.

In November 1664 the Welsh buccaneer Captain Morris Williams sent a note to Modyford. He offered to come in to Port Royal with a rich Spanish prize ship containing indigo, precious logwoods and silver, if security was given that it could be used to pay off his debts in Jamaica. Modyford refused to give him any promises, and Williams sailed in eight days later. The goods were seized, and the

In April 1666, Williams took the 16-gun *Speaker* and with Edward Morgan sacked Saint Eustatius and Saba (see Edward Morgan). The English had received news that the Second Anglo-Dutch War had started. Morgan boarded Williams' *Speaker* as his flagship and set sail with five ships, another flotilla of 3 ships following on behind. Modyford wrote that there were about 650 men in the invasion force, '*chiefly reformed privateers, scarce a planter amongst them, being resolute fellows and well*

*1684 'Bucaniers of America' – mainly about Henry Morgan by a man who sailed under him*

armed with fusils (muskets) and pistols.' The Governor was pleased that the men went 'at the old rate of no purchase, no pay, and it will cost the King nothing considerable, some powder and mortar pieces.'

## COLONEL BLEDRI MORGAN fl. 1660

A kinsman of Henry Morgan, he was one of the most important buccaneers in Jamaica between 1660 and 1670. He commanded the rearguard of 300 men at the taking of Panama in 1670. In May 1671 he was appointed as Deputy-Governor of Providence Island by Sir James Modyford.

## LIEUTENANT-COLONEL EDWARD MORGAN d. 1664

This buccaneer from a noble Welsh family was the uncle of Henry, so giving the lie to the claim that Henry was an indentured servant on his arrival in the Indies. He served as a mercenary in the 30 Years War in Germany, and married the daughter of the mayor of Lippstadt. In the English Civil War, he was a Royalist Colonel, and after the execution of Charles I, Morgan went into exile in Germany. On the Restoration of the Monarchy, he was named Lieutenant-Governor of Jamaica,

DE
AMERICAENSCHE
ZEE-ROOVERS
Behelsende een Partinent
Verhael van alle de Roverye
En Onmenscliycke Wreet-
heeden die de Engelsche
en Franse Roovers
Tegens de Spanjaerden
in America
Gepleeght
Hebben.

t'Amsterdam by JAN ten HOORN, Boeckverkoper
Over het Oude Heerelogement - 1678

*Two of the central pictures depict Morgan's men*

In 1665, when the Dutch declared war on England (The Second Dutch War), Governor Modyford commissioned Morgan to command a privateer's fleet against the French. Modyford gave commissions to the assembled pirates and buccaneers to attack the Dutch islands of St Eustacius (now St Kitt's, or St Christopher's Island), Saba, Tobago and Curacao.

Edward Morgan had been given command of 10 ships and 500 men, most of them '*reformed prisoners*', and including some condemned pirates who were reprieved and pardoned for the expedition. The crews mutinied before leaving Jamaica, but were pacified by the offer of an equal share of the spoils. Nine ships eventually met at Pinos Island, but there was disagreement on Morgan's plan of attack. Three ships deserted to attack Virginia, but the rest of the fleet sailed on to St Eustatius, arriving on 23rd July, 1665. Morgan, by now old and corpulent, collapsed during the fighting and died of a heart attack. His vice-commander Theodore Cary forced the Dutch colonists to choose between accepting English rule, or leaving the island. A small military force was left on the nearby island of Nevis.

deputy to Sir Thomas Modyford, arriving in the West Indies in the summer of 1664.

## LIEUTENANT-COLONEL THOMAS MORGAN fl. 1665-1685

He sailed with Edward Morgan, and was left in charge of St Eustatia and Saba after they had been captured in 1665. In 1686 he commanded a company of buccaneers responding to a plea from Governor Wells of St Kitts, who was being attacked by the French. In a pathetic defence of the island, only Morgan's company emerged with credit, and Morgan was shot in both legs.

## CAPTAIN WILLIAM JAMES fl. 1660-1663

A buccaneer operating off Jamaica and Tortuga, Governor D'Oyley of Jamaica gave him a 'let pass' for his frigate *America* in May 1660. In 1663 James was in command of 70 men on the 6-gun frigate, on Commodore Myng's expedition to Campeachy, leaving Port Royal in January. However, Captain Mitchell in the *Blessing*, wrote that he failed to reach Campeachy: '*about 90 leagues this side of Campeche, he met three sail of the fleet, viz. Captain William James his ship, sunk in the sea by foul weather, who was the next best ship in the fleet to the Admiral (Maynos), and that many of their men in the fleet were dead.*'

It appears that James was the buccaneer who discovered the true value of logwood for the privateers. '*Captain James carried off a Spanish prize full of logwood, being astonished upon reaching port at the high price his cargo fetched.*' Until then, however, he had '*known so little of its real value that he had burned much of it for fuel on the voyage*' to England. The '*Brethren of the Coast*' now started illicit logging operations along the Campeche coast, the Bay of Honduras and in Mexico's Laguna de Terminos.

## CAPTAIN JOHN JAMES fl. 1699

This Welshman commanded a pirate brigantine around Madagascar, and sometimes sailed with Ort Van Tyle, the New York merchant/privateer. Sailing in American waters in the galley *Alexander*, with Thomas Howard, later a noted pirate, as one of his crew, he had formerly plundered Atlantic shipping. It appears that he took up with Captain William Read on a 60-ton brig, transferring his galley's guns. A 200-ton ship was taken in the Persian Gulf, and in their eagerness to search for gold, threw a bale of trade goods overboard, in which had been hidden a great quantity of the metal. Read died, and James took over the 'small, crazy and worm-eaten brig', heading for Mayotte. Here they laid up, taking the mast out of the brig, and adding it to the one-masted 200-ton prize (a ship known as a grab). The new brig was given the name of James' former *Alexander*. Abandoning the old brig, provisions were taken on, and the pirates found a 12-oared boat, which had been washed ashore when the *Ruby* East -India Man had been lost at sea.

They remained at Mayotte for six months, over the monsoon season, then sailed for Madagascar. James chased a French ship, and soon discovered it was also a pirate. '*They hailed each other, and received the same answer from each vessel, viz. "From the Seas"*', so the ships joined forces. Captain Fourgette's ship, laden with liquor from Martinique, had been taken by George Booth at Ambonavoula. Fourgette had been intending to swap the alcohol for slaves with the pirates in Madagascar, but fooled by Booth. Booth and James now sailed together. 70 or 80 men of James' crew were taken on by the pirate Captain White's *Speaker* in Madagascar. Also the *Alexander's* guns were transferred to the *Speaker* at St Augustin Bay, so one can only assume that the ship was in poor condition. What happened to John James is unknown.

## CAPTAIN EVAN JONES fl. 1699

This pirate flashes through history at Port Dauphin in the Indian Ocean, when he pulled into port and looted an American slaver. He gave the ship to Abraham Samuel, the mulatto pirate and self-styled '*King of Port Dauphin, Tollannare, Farrawe, Fanquest and Fownzahira*'. Samuel sold it to four pirates from 1,100 pieces of eight.

## ROBERT EDWARDS fl. 1690-1720 – *The Privateer who Owned Manhattan*

The Welsh privateer Robert Edwards was given 77 acres of what is now the heart of Manhattan, by Queen Anne for his services in for raiding Spanish galleons loaded down with treasure from the New World. (She reigned from 1702-1707). His will gave the area to the Cruger brothers, on a 99-year lease, with the understanding that it would revert back to his heirs after that. Somehow the land ended up in the hands of Trinity Church, one of New York's biggest landowners. The land is valued at $680 billion, and includes the site of the World Trade Centre, Broadway and Wall Street). Robert Edwards died childless, leaving his property to his sister in Wales and her descendants who are estimated now to number 5,400. Evidence uncovered at the Public Record Office at Kew, proved that Edwards existed and owned land in New York in the late 1690s. Robert Edwards may have been born in Llanmynech, arriving in New York in the late 1690s. His descendants believe he was given 77 acres of prime land by the British Crown. They say he – or his sons – leased this land to church wardens of Trinity Church, now a big real estate owner in New York. Land grants in New York in the 18th century are difficult to trace. In the case of the Edwards' family claim, it may be that the cross-dressing Colonel Fletcher, Governor of New York, was informed that was about to be sacked and so gave away every part of the city that he could lay his hands on. Trinity Church disputes the claims of the heirs, relying upon the statute of limitations, whereby a claim must be made within 15 years of the start of the dispute. However, the heirs believe they can overturn the statute, if they are able to demonstrate there was an error in the way in which the leases were handed over. There are records in the National Archives and masses of material upon the net, for anyone wishing to research this intriguing case.

## CAPTAIN JOHN BOWEN d. 1704

Some sources call Bowen a Rhode Islander of Welsh descent, but he was born in Bermuda, possibly the son of one of the Royalist prisoners captured at the Battle of St Ffagans by the Parliamentarians in the Second Civil War. Moving to South Carolina, John Bowen became captain of a merchant vessel trading with the West Indies, but after some years was captured by French pirates. The French crossed the Atlantic to pillage the West African slave-coast, then went around the Cape to the island of Madagascar. Here they were ship-wrecked, and around eighteen months later Bowen and a few other survivors were picked up by the pirate Captain Read.

Read took a huge Arab ship in the Persian Gulf, but with little loot aboard, and around this time Bowen signed pirates' articles, despairing of ever returning to the Americas. He was now elected sailing-master, on account of his experience, and with Read, sailed in consort with the pirate captain George Booth off Western Madagascar. At the end of 1699, the two ships captured the *Speaker*, a strong 50-gun slave ship at Mathelage (now Majunga) off Madagascar's northwest coast. Booth now led the three ships and over 200 pirates to Zanzibar for supplies. In a quarrel with Arab soldiers, Booth and 20 pirates were killed there in late 1700. John Bowen was elected captain of the *Speaker* in his place. Bowen now took several ships off the Malabar coast in 1700, trading the goods in local towns.

Near the mouth of the Red Sea, Bowen took an Indian ship with £100,000 worth of booty in 1701 According to Jan Rogozinski, its value would be $50 million today. In November 1701, the *Speaker* took an English East Indiaman off Callequilon (Quilon), which was then sold on the Indian coast. According to Defoe, its Captain Conway had sailed from Bengal, and the loot was divided equally and sold to a Callequillon merchant, a merchant of Porca and a Dutch factor named Malpa. Returning to Madagascar, on January 7th,

1702 Bowen's ship was wrecked on St Thomas Reef off Mauritius, but most of the loot and crew were saved. Bowen gave Governor Roelof Deodati a huge bribe of 2,500 pieces of eight, for which he was warmly welcomed, and allowed to buy a replacement vessel. Bowen also gave the governor the wreck of the *Speaker*, with its stores and guns. The governor provided doctors, medicine and food to the shipwrecked pirates. Bowen bought and converted a Dutch sloop into a brigantine, and in the middle of March left the island, leaving the Governor a generous gift. (It appears that the remains of the *Speaker* have been found).

Defoe's account reads: *Then* [the Speaker] *left the coast and sailed for the island of Madagascar, but in the way was lost on the island of Mauritius, on St Thomas's Reef, where they were most courteously received and feasted, their sick carried into their fort and cured by their doctor, and a new sloop sold them. And* [they were] *supplied with all sorts of necessaries for their cutting her* (*the Sloop*) *and making her a brigantine, which they performed in the middle of March 1702 and took their leave of the Governor, giving him 2,500 pieces of eight ... and being invited to make Mauritius a place of refreshment, sailed for the island of Madagascar, where at a place on the east side, called Maritan* [St Mary's] *the captain with a gang settled themselves.*' The wrecked *Speaker* had held 170 pirates and 30 Indian captives, but the sloop would not hold as many crew, so all the Indians and 12 seamen were left behind in Mauritius. Arriving at the French island of Réunion, several French pirates left the crowded ship. In return, a few settlers joined the pirates and sailed on to St Mary's.

In April 1702, Bowen returned to Madagascar via Réunion, and set up a camp at Maritan (St Mary's) on its eastern coast, where he built a fort. Governor Villiers recorded his arrival at Réunion on April 2nd. Bowen then took the *Speedy Return*, belonging to the Scottish Company of Africa, which had stopped to provision at Maritan, after taking on slaves at St Mary's. It was accompanied by the East India Company's *Content*, a brigantine also carrying slaves. Bowen and his men rowed up to the anchored ships at night, and took them with ease, overpowering the sleeping crew. Most of the 50 or so crew off the ships joined the pirates.

Captain Drummond of the *Speedy Return* and Captain Stewart of the *Content* were released at St Mary's, and both seem to have died on the island. The loss of the *Speedy Return* was blamed upon Captain Thomas Green and the crew of the Scottish ship *Worcester*, which was trading along the Malabar Coast at this time. On its return to Scotland, Green and 17 of his crew were convicted of massacring the *Speedy Return*'s crew. Green and two others were hanged in 1705, before the error was realised and the rest of the crew pardoned. Israel Phipenny and Peter Freeland, two of Bowen's forced men, had escaped at Mauritius and had arrived in Portsmouth in March 1705. By the time the Mayor of Portsmouth had reported their affidavits to the secretary of State in London, and the Secretary had sent pardons by Express Coach to Scotland, poor Green had been dead for just a few hours.

Bowen now left Maritan with the *Speedy Return* and *Content*, having heard from Drummond's crew that Captain Honeycomb's galley *Rook* was lying at Mascarenas Bay, but it had left just before their arrival. Next, Bowen's consort brigantine ran aground off the west coast of Madagascar. It was refloated and caught up with the *Speedy Return* at Augustine Bay in Madagascar, but was so badly damaged that the pirates burnt it. In October 1702, the *Speaker* added the English ship *Borneo* to their list of Indian vessels captured, and used several Indian and European merchants along the Malabar coast to trade their booty.

Next, Bowen sailed from New Methelage to Johanna and finally to Mayotte (Mayota), where he linked forces with Thomas Howard, captain of the *Prosperous*, around Christmas 1702. Bowen failed to capture the French ship *Corbel* after a chase, and headed for Mauritius, and then for the East Indies. The two ships took and looted a rich English East Indiaman, the *Pembroke* on March 10th 1703 at Mayotte. It was unfortunately stuck in its anchorage, and thus defenceless. Its captain had anchored her where the bay became dry when the tide ebbed. Bowen's men in two small boats approached her and asked to come aboard. '*Captain Weoley answered one of them might come only. Yet they both came rowing on and when they came under our quarter all their men at once started up with their arms guarded* [ready to fire] *swearing if any of us fired a shot they would do us no harm nor take anything from us. Captain Weoley ordered everyone to fire, which we did, and they at us ... but we were not able to keep up with them, they firing six shot to our one ... so we called for quarters which they gave, disarming every man and turning them into the head.*' The *Pembroke* was looted, but the crew unusually voted not to burn her, although four pirates had been killed in the attack, along with the *Pembroke's* Chief Mate and another sailor.

Bowen kept the *Pembroke's* Captain Whalley (or Wooley) until October to serve as a pilot. (Whalley's letter to Mr Penning, head of the New East India Company of Calicut, sent in November 1703, gave Defoe his background information on John Bowen). The two pirate captains now separated, for Bowen to careen the *Speedy Return*, but rejoined a few months later in the Red Sea. Whaley wrote that the pirates went to Mathelage, returned to the Comoros and then sailed to the Highland of St Johns. In August 1703 Bowen and Howard took two Indian ships (returning to Surat from Mocha), worth £70,000 in the Red Sea, and some Moorish prizes. Howard's *Prosperous* took one and left it adrift off Daman without an anchor, and Bowen's *Speedy Return* took a larger ship and carried it to Rajapura in India. They shared the loot at Rajapura, and burned the *Prosperous* and *Speedy Return*, as they had become unsound. The captains converted Bowen's Indian prize, named it the *Defiance*, and set off in October 1703 with 56 guns and 164 pirates for the Malabar Coast. There were 50 Frenchmen, 43 Englishmen, and a mixture of Danes, Swedes and Dutchmen. 60 captured Indian crew were kept on board to perform menial tasks. According to Jan Rogozinski, the value of the two Indian ships was $100 million in today's money. Even after sharing this with Howard, it would mean that Bowen had taken the equivalent of $100 million in two years off Indian ships.

North of Cochin on the Malabar Coast to dispose of their goods, the *Defiance* '*anchored and fired several guns. But no boat coming off, the quartermaster* [John North] *went near the shore, and had conference by boat with the people, who next day brought off hogs and other refreshments ... There came several Dutchmen aboard, and I saw no difference between their treatment of the pirates and any other ship.*' Here they came again upon the unfortunate *Pembroke*, and once again ransacked her. The pirates next put into North-West Harbour in Dutch-controlled, friendly Mauritius. Howard had remained with his men on the Indian coast, while Bowen sailed for the Mascarenes with 40 of his crew, intending to return home with their booty and escape piracy. According to Defoe, Howard and twenty of his crew were left on the Indian coast '*with what they had, and retired among the Natives, where Howard married a Woman of the country, and being a morose ill-natured Fellow, and using her ill, he was murdered by her Relations.*'

John Bowen sailed the *Defiance* to Mauritius and Réunion in February and April 1704. Six men left at Mauritius to retire. Bowen and several others were accepted as settlers at Réunion. Some of the French pirates who left Bowen's command at Réunion were Guy Dumesnil, Joseph de Guigne*, George Christmas and Pierra Pradau. They were said to have been taken back to France by Baron de Pallieres' squadron in 1705. Unluckily, Bowen fell ill with an intestinal complaint, and died there after about six months in March 1705. '*The dry Belly ache*' which carried Bowen off may have been the '*dry gripes*', contracted by drinking rum held in lead containers. His goods were seized by the church and he was refused a Christian burial. He was known as '*Jean Bouin*' on the island. Bowen was succeeded by Nathaniel North as captain of the *Challenge*. According to Gosse, Bowen had accumulated over a million dollars in coin, plus vast quantities of valuable merchandise. The East India Company seized the fortune that he left behind. About 200 of Bowen's men stayed on the *Defiance* and sailed on to St Mary's Island (just off the east coast of Madagascar), now under a former quartermaster, Nathaniel North.

* Joseph de Guigne, who disembarked at Réunion, had served Bowen on the *Speaker*, *Speedy Return* and the *Defiance* from 1697 – 1704. He was recorded as marrying on the island in November 1704, and later used his booty to buy land in three separate locations on Réunion.

## NOTE ON THOMAS HOWARD, WHO SAILED WITH BOWEN

His nationality is unknown, but he may have been a Welshman who squandered his inheritance, and fled to Jamaica to escape his creditors. With some other seamen, he took a canoe, then took a small boat, then a sloop, gradually building up to taking a 24-gun ship, where he was elected quartermaster. In 1698 he was active off the North American coast, then crossed to the West African coast to plunder more ships.

However, the ship ran onto a reef off Madagascar in 1700. Most of the crew started ferrying heavier cargo off the ship to lighten it, and Howard took over the boat and sailed off with all the treasure. He was then abandoned ashore while hunting, until joining Captain George Booth. Booth had been a gunner on the *Pelican*, then the *Dolphin* from 1696, and had been trapped at St Mary's Island by the Royal Navy. The *Dolphin* was burned, but Booth had escaped to Madagascar with most of his men. The pirates seized a French ship which had put in to barter liquor and goods for slaves, and then met up with John Bowen.

In April 1700, Bowen and Booth took the *Speaker*, a 50-gun 450-ton slaver. Picking up provisions in Zanzibar, George Booth was attacked and killed by Arab troops, and John Bowen became captain. Bowen wrecked the *Speaker* in 1701, when Howard left him, returning to Madagascar and staying at St Augustine's Bay. Howard now seized the 36-gun *Prosperous*, was elected captain and rejoined with Bowen in consort in 1702. The pair looted the *Pembroke* at Johanna Island (Anjouan) in the Comoros in March 1703. In August, the pirates again met up in the Red Sea, taking two Indian ships and over £70,000 in treasure. Dividing the loot at Rajapura, India, both Bowen's crew and Howard's men transferred to the largest Indian ship. Howard retired, and was killed by his in-laws, as noted above.

## DAVID WILLIAMS fl. 1698-1709

The son of a Welsh farmer, he was more of a soldier than a pirate. He was recorded as being a morose character, who '*knew as little of the sea or of ships as he did of the Arts of natural Philosophy*'. A seaman on a merchant ship bound for India, probably the *Mary*, an East Indiaman out of Bristol, he was accidentally left on Madagascar. Williams found employment in fighting for native chiefs in an inter-tribal battle. He fought so well that he was befriended by the 'King', but a short time later this tribe was wiped out and Williams was taken prisoner. The King of this tribe, knowing of Williams' reputation, made him leader of his army, but Williams was again captured, by a King named Dempaino. He was made commander-in-chief of an army of 6,000 men, and supplied with slaves, expensive clothing and all his needs.

Escaping, he sailed on the Rhode Island privateer *Pelican* in 1698, and then joined the Mocha under Robert Culliford, possibly around May 1698, when Culliford was at St Mary's Island off Madagascar. Culliford took £2,000 in cash from a French ship there (to add to his previous tally of other European, Indonesian and Chinese captures), and took on about a hundred of the crew of his former captain, William Kidd. Culliford now sailed off in the Mocha, with Dirk Chivers' *Soldado* and the *Pelican*. Chivers and Culliford plundered the Great Mohamed in the Red Sea in September 1698. There was

£130,000 in cash, each crewman receiving £700. Another prize was taken, and the ships sailed to St Mary's in February 1699.

In September 1699, the crew of the *Mocha* split up at Madagascar, sinking the *Mocha* when four British warships arrived. All of the 24 pirates, who took the offer of a pardon from the naval commander, seem to have been hanged in London, except for Chivers and Culliford. Culliford was kept alive to testify against Samuel Burgess. At Madagascar, Williams had not trusted the pardon offer, and instead helped George Booth take a French ship. Booth's *Dolphin* was trapped at St Mary's Island in 1699, and burned, but its crew escaped to Madagascar. They then joined up with Williams' fellow-Welshman John Bowen (q.v.), and Williams sailed on the *Speaker* until it was wrecked in 1701. He returned to Madagascar, and joined Thomas Howard's *Prosperous* in 1702. However, he was accidentally left behind when Howard attacked a Dutch trader on the island.

According to Gosse, and details are entangled here, he was captured by the Dutch pirate Ort Van Tyle, who was sailing out on New York. Van Tyle was an associate of the Welsh pirate Captain James, and they both roamed the coasts off Madagascar and the Indian Ocean. He put his prisoners to work on his Madagascar plantation as slaves, and David Williams toiled there for 6 months before making his escape to a friendly tribe in the neighbourhood. He lived with Prince Rebaiharang's tribe for a year, then joined a Dutchman named Pro, who had a small settlement on the island. Williams was now arrested by a naval frigate, the *HMS Severn* in November 1703, but escaped with Pro, procuring a boat from the Comoro Islands in February 1704. The *Severn* and the *Scarborough* had been sent at the request of the East India Company of a 'search and destroy' mission against the pirates infesting the waters around Madagascar.

Williams now joined Thomas White's pirates at Methalage, in Madagascar, and became Captain White's quartermaster in 1704. White had been captured with John Bowen back in 1698, and had been Thomas Howard's quartermaster. Williams was present when several more ships were taken in the Red Sea, as White sailed in consort with Captain Halsey, before dying of fever. White had married a local woman of Methelage, and died in her arms in 1708, reportedly of '*excessive drinking and other irregularities*'. A Bostonian, Halsey had a commission to raid French and Spanish shipping in 1704, but turned from privateer to pirate in 1705, taking the 10-gun *Charles* to Madagascar. In 1706, he was deposed by pirate council for cowardice, when he refused to attack a large Dutch ship. However, when the Dutch ship attacked the *Charles*, he was quickly reinstated as captain.

Williams became John Halsey's quartermaster in 1707, making a fortune. Two coastal merchant ships were taken in February 1707 at the Nicobar Islands. At Mocha, in the Red sea, in August 1707, the pirates attacked a fleet of five British ships, with a total of 62 guns. The fleet scattered, but Halsey took two of the vessels, with £50,000 worth of cash and cargo. In January 1708, the *Greyhound* arrived at Madagascar to trade alcohol and other provisions for the provisions taken from the British prizes. The *Neptune* also arrived in port to trade in liquor. However, a hurricane wrecked the pirate ships and their prizes. With the assistance of Samuel Burgess, first mate on the Scottish ship *Neptune*, and a former privateer, the pirates took over the *Neptune* and plundered the *Greyhound*. (Captain Culliford, the pirate, had testified against Burgess in his London trial, but Burgess was mysteriously pardoned in 1702). Halsey became captain of the *Neptune*, and Burgess quartermaster, as his reward. On Halsey's death from fever in 1708, Burgess was voted out as quartermaster, and Williams became the captain of the *Neptune*, but another hurricane wrecked the ship before he could leave Madagascar. Undeterred, Williams and ten pirates fitted out a small sloop, and sailed for Mascarenas Island.

Missing the island, they sailed around Madagascar to Mathelage, where Williams laid the boat up for a year, dealing in slaves with Burgess and others. The local king, annoyed by Williams' irrational outbursts of temper, ordered him to leave, but prevailing winds meant that Williams could not reach his intended destination on the north of the island, but was forced into the port of Boyne, just a few miles from Mathelage, and still within the king's realm. Boyne was noted for its Arabian trade, and Williams anchored offshore, intending to see its Arab Governor. He took a canoe inshore and asked for directions to Kings Town, but an ambush had been laid. Defoe states that his 13-year pirate career came to an end in 1709: '*When they had left the Boyne, Williams and Meyeurs, a Frenchman, who also came ashore in the canoe, went to buy some Samsams, which are agate beads; and as they were looking over these goods, a number of the Governor's Men came about them, seized them both and immediately dispatched Meyeurs, Williams they bound, and tortured almost a whole day, by throwing hot Ashes on his Head and in his Face, and putting little Boys to beat him with Sticks; he offered the Governor $2000 for his life, but he answered he'd have both that and the money too; and accordingly when he was near expiring, they made an end of him with lances.*' Williams' friend and benefactor, King Dempaino, revenged his death by sacking the Arab town and executing its chief with lances. Burgess had stayed in Madagascar and dealt in slaves with Williams and other captains, but was poisoned by a black chief after an argument over prices.

## TOM COLLINS fl. 1695-1715

He appears to have been first a member of '*Long John*' Avery's crew, probably arriving at Madagascar on the *Charming Mary* in 1695, and then ending his career by taking up slaving. Sailing for Captain Thomas White, Collins is also mentioned as one of Captain Booth's men by Defoe: '*As soon as the purser was ashore, he was taken Prisoner, by one Tom Collins, a Welchman born in Pembrokeshire, who lived on Shore, and had belonged to the Charming Mary of Barbadoes, which went out with a Commission, but was converted to a Pyrate; he told the Purser, he was his Prisoner, and must answer the Damage done to two Merchants, who were slaving ... He was carried by Collins on board Booth's ship ...*' Collins will have met the Welsh Captain Bowen (q.v.) at this juncture of his career. He was with Captain David Williams (q.v.) at Madagascar, captured by Ort Van Tyle when Thomas Howard tried to imprison the Dutchman. Both Welshmen, Collins with his arm broken, were forced to work as slaves for van Tyle. Collins controlled a great deal of the slave trade on the east coast in the years around 1715.

## CAPTAIN HENRY JENNINGS fl. 1714

According to Gosse, '*this Welsh pirate had been a man of good position, education, and property before he took to piracy, which he did for the love of the life and not from necessity.*' In 1714, the Spanish treasure fleet carrying the Royal taxes back to Spain ran into a hurricane, and was run aground on the shallow reefs of Florida. While the Spanish were attempting salvage operations, Jennings attacked and robbed the poorly defended salvage divers. He then established his base in Nassau in New Providence, where he could elude the Spanish navy. The harbour had two entrances, making it difficult for a single man-of-war to '*bottle up*' the port. There was ample fresh water, fish, turtle and wild game. The island was positioned ideally between the westbound shipping lanes carrying needed provisions from Europe, and the eastbound lanes taking gold and silver to Europe. Jennings was soon joined by other pirate captains, and a community of two-thousand soon formed, living on ships, and in tents and huts. A Captain Stone, who was taken by Jennings, noted that he treated him civilly and stated that he would not harm Englishmen. Jennings' crew restricted their looting to 20 gallons of rum, for which they paid him handsomely.

Held in high esteem by his fellows in the Bahamas, becoming the unofficial Mayor of Nassau, and he presided at the meeting in 1717 when pirates gathered to discuss King George's offer of a pardon. Jennings was reported to have offered the new Governor of the Bahamas, Woodes Rogers 10% of all profits on the island, instead of the normal 8%, for looking the other way, but Rogers could not be tempted. After much discussion, Jennings declared that he would take up the king's offer of pardon, and around 150 other pirates then followed him in declaring the same intention. On the new Governor's arrival from England they received pardon certificates, although Johnson reflected that most of them returned to their evil ways, '*like a Dog to the Vomit.*' Jennings' main ally in accepting the pardon and working with Governor Rogers, was Captain Benjamin Hornigold, who had taught Blackbeard piracy, and who then sailed with Paulsgrave Williams and Sam Bellamy. Hornigold later turned into a notable 'pirate-chaser'.

## WILLIAM LEWIS d. 1718

This Captain Lewis appears in Johnson's *General History of the Pyrates*. William Lewis was a former prize-fighter who operated from New Providence in the Bahamas. When Woodes Rogers offered the King's Pardon in July 1718, he accepted it. Like Howell Davies, he was sent by Rogers to trade for food in October, and like Davies, he mutinied. Three sloops were commanded by John Auger, Henry White and William Greenway, all pardoned pirates. Two days out from New Providence, yet another pardoned pirate, Phineas Bunce, led the mutiny at anchor off Green Cay, assisted by Lewis. Auger needed no convincing to join them, but Greenway was forced. They stripped Captain White and seven other crew members naked and marooned them on Green Cay. Several times over the next few weeks the pirates visited the islet, beating up the men, until they were rescued seven weeks later.

The three sloops were comprehensively beaten in a fight with the Spanish costagarda at Long Island. Captain Phineas Bunce was wounded in battle and captured, but died before he could be hanged. Auger and around 15 men escaped ashore, but were recaptured by Benjamin Hornigold. Another ring-leader of the mutiny, and yet another former pardoned pirate, was Dennis McCarthy. Wishing to be hanged in style at New Providence, in front of his former colleagues in piracy, he put on clean linen, tied his cap, neck, wrists and knees with long blue ribbons, and stepped onto the scaffold. He kicked off his shoes, having sworn not to die with his boots on. Also showing no remorse at the gallows, William Lewis asked for alcohol to toast his fellow prisoners and the crown in 1718. Defoe records '*William Lewis, aged about 34 Years, as he had been a hardy Pyrate and Prize-Fighter, affected an Unconcern at Death; but heartily desired Liquors to drink with his Sufferers on the Stage, and with the Standers by.*' And of another Welshman hung with Lewis he records '*Thomas Morris, aged about 22, had been a very incorrigible Youth and Pyrate, and seemed to have very little Anxiety of Mind by his frequent Smiles when at the Bar, being dressed with red ribbons as Macarhty was in blue, he said, going over the Ramparts, "We have a new Governor, but a harsh one", and a little before he was turned off, said aloud, that he might have been a greater Plague to these Islands, and now wished he had been so.*'

Captain Hornigold is particularly noteworthy in that he was the captain of Edward Teach (Blackbeard). He gave Blackbeard a captured sloop, and they sailed in consort from New Providence. In 1717 they took six ships of the coast of the North American colonies, then returned to the Caribbean, capturing a huge French ship laden with gold and jewels. Blackbeard took his share of the booty and adopted the prize as his ship, while the wealthy Hornigold returned to New Providence. There, he not only accepted the King's pardon, but became friendly with the new Governor of the Bahamas, Woodes Rogers, from July 1718. Among other pirates he captured Auger and William Lewis, before being sent by Rogers to Mexico, where his ship foundered on a hidden reef in 1719.

Note:

There was also a James Lewis, who was taken prisoner by the French, escaped to Spain and joined Captain 'Long Ben' Avery to capture the *Charles the Second*. Tried at the Old Bailey, he was hung in 1696.

## JOHN WILLIAMS fl. 1718

The only note we have of his life is important, as it shows that Bart Roberts was a pirate prior to being captured by Howell Davis. In 1737 Clement Downing wrote the life of John Plantain in his *A compendious history of the Indian wars*. Downing was in the naval ship *King George*, in conflict with Angria around 1717-1722, and knew of Roberts, Plantain and Edward England being pirates in the area. '*He* [John Plantain] *followed this Course of Life till he was near 20 Years of Age, when he came to Rhode-Island; there he fell into company with several Men who belonged to a Pyrate Sloop. These try'd to persuade him, with several others, to go with them; shewing great Sums of Gold, and treating him and others in a profuse and expensive Manner. His own wicked Inclinations soon led him to accept the Offer, without much Hesitation. At the same time, he acknowledged that he had no Occasion to go with them, as he belonged to a very honest Commander, and one that used the Sailors very well on all Accounts. But being of a roving Disposition, he could not bear being under any Restraint They soon went on board this Pyrate Sloop, and were entertained in a handsome manner, being presented to the*

Captain, who seem'd to like them very well, and told them if they would sail with him, they should have the same Encouragement as the other People had, and that they mould in a short time take a Voyage which would prove the making of them all; after this they design'd to accept the first Act of Grace, and leave off.

They left Rhode-Island in this Sloop which they called the Terrible, commanded by John Williams; and one Roberts being a bold and resolute Man, was made Quarter-master. With John Plantain entered the following five, viz John James of Boston in New England and Henry Millis of Falmouth in the Weft of England; Richard Dean of Stepney in London; John Harvey of Shadwell; and Henry Jones of St Pauls London; all young Men, the oldest not being above 23 Years of Age. Whenever any enter on board of these Ships voluntarily, they are obliged to sign all their Articles of Agreement; which is in effect, to renounce Honour, and all human Condition, for they seldom shew any Mercy to those who fall into their Hands. Frome Rhode-Island and they shaped their Course for the Coast of Guinea, and in their way took three Ships, amongst the Crews of which was Mr. Moore the Surgeon, spoken of in the Account of Commodore Matthews's Transactions.

They pretended to give Liberty to those Ships Crews either to go or stay with them. The Boatswain of the Ship to which Mr. Moore belonged entered voluntarily, and would have used his Captain and several of the Men very barbarously, but [Black Bart] Roberts who was then Quarter-master, would not allow of it. They kept the Surgeon and Carpenter by Compulsion, when they found they chose to leave them; and took one of the Ships, which prov'd to be the best Sailor, and called her the Defiance. Now they had got a Ship of near 300 Tuns, which mounted 30 Guns, well mann'd and well stored with Provisions. They usually are at no certain Allowance amongst themselves, till they are in a Likelihood of being short of Provision, but every Man is allowed to eat what he pleases.

Then they put all under the care of their Quarter-master, who discharges all things with an Equality to them all, every Man and Boy faring alike; and even their Captain, or any other Officer, is allowed no more than another Man; nay, the Captain cannot keep his own Cabbin to himself, for their Bulk heads are all down, and every Man stands to his Quarters, where they lie and mess [eat], tho' they take the liberty of ranging all over the Ships. This large Ship they took was bound for Jamaica, called the Prosperous of London one Capt. James Commander; whom, and so many of his Crew as were not willing to go with them, they put on board those two other Vessels they let go. The Prosperous had on board a considerable number of East-India Bales, which they hoisted up on Deck, and slit open; the Quarter-master distributing the fame amongst the Pyrates.

They arrived in a short time on the Coast of Guinea and kept all the trading Ships from carrying on any manner of Commerce at Gambo, and the other Ports on that Coast. Here they met with the Onslow whom they fought a considerable time; but the Pyrates being well mann'd, boarding her, made sad Havock of her Crew, and brought them to cry out for Quarter, which is but very indifferent at best; so when they had taken her, they made one of their number whose Name was [Edward] England a Man who had been Mate of several good Ships, Captain of her. Plantain and his Companions were daily increasing their Store; for not long after they took the Onslow they mastered a Dutch Interloper, with whom they had a smart Battle, and had not the Sloop come to their Assistance, they would have been obliged to let her go. But the Sloop coming up, and pouring a great number of Men on board, they soon over-powered them. This Ship they liked exceeding well, and were resolved to keep her, calling her the Fancy and Capt. England having a mind to her, they allowed him to command her. They daily now increased their number, and were not for keeping so many Ships, imagining they should soon have a Squadron of Men of War after them, which they did not care to have any Correspondence with.

Now Capt. England proposed a new Voyage to them, which might be the making of them all very rich; and as they had got such good Ships under their Command, they were resolved to make the best of their present Situation. First they proposed to burn the Terrible Sloop, being old and leaky, and not fit to beat about the Cape, So having finished their Cruise on the Coast of Guinea they were resolved to steer another way. These Pyrates had now got the Fancy under the Command of Capt. England and a small Brigantine called the Unity which they named the Expedition and gave the Command to one Johnson that was with them, tho' one Quarter-matter serv'd for them all. And being in great Dispute how and which way they

*Captain Lewis giving a lock of hair to the Devil*

should dispose of each other, they went on shore on the Coast of Guinea and there held a fresh Consultation, when some were for going with Capt. England and some with Capt. Roberts.

These Disputes lasted for some time, but it was left to a committee to choose from among them, on whose Determination they resolved to rely. They had now six or seven Ships with them, on which account it was resolved, that England and Roberts should separate, for fear of a Civil War amongst themselves. England was to take the Fancy, the Snow, and the Ship they called the Victory, and go away for the East Indies; and Roberts and the rest were to continue and range about those Seas, as they thought fit. Roberts afterwards fell into the Hands of Sir Chaloner Ogle, and by him was brought to Justice, and he and his Crew were hung up in Chains along the Coast of Guinea, from Cape-Coast-Castle. Capt. England took to the Eastern Seas, and came away for St. Augustine's Bay, on the Island of Madagascar...' We shall see that Black Bart Roberts was not hung, and that Edward England assisted Howell Davis into piracy. Somehow, by Spring 1719 Roberts was third mate on a slaver, having abandoned piracy for a few weeks.

## HOWELL DAVIS c. 1690-19 June 1719 – '*The Cavalier Prince of Pirates*'

The career of this pirate is one of the more interesting of Defoe's case studies – he met some of the pirates who served with Davis and Black Bart Roberts, and Davis is recorded in far more detail in this author's biography of Black Bart. Born in Milford Haven, Pembrokeshire, Davis was first mate aboard Captain Skinner's Bristol slaver *Cadogan*, which was taken off Sierra Leone by Edward England on 11 July 1718. Although the *Cadogan* surrendered, Skinner was pelted with broken bottles and shot dead by some of England's men. Skinner was a brutal man, who had previously dismissed them without pay from a voyage after a disagreement. The remaining men on the Cadogan were given the option to turn pirate and sign England's articles. Davis refused, saying he would rather be shot.

England was impressed by his bravery and gave him back command of the *Cadogan*, allowing him to sail off on 18 July. England had instructed him to set sail for a certain latitude, and then open a sealed letter, which contained a deed of gift of the ship and its cargo to Davis and his crew. They were told to sail to Brazil, where the cargo could be sold and the profits shared equally. However, the crew mutinied and took the *Cadogan* to Barbados, and Davis was thrown into jail for piracy. After 3 months, Davis was released for lack of evidence, but ship-owners now refused to employ him. Davis thus went to Nassau, where its new governor, Woodes Rogers, took pity on him, offering Davis a place on board the merchant sloop *Buck*. The *Buck* sailed in consort for Martinique with the *Mumvil Trader* and the *Samuel*, with many of the crews being pirates pardoned by Rogers. Anchored off Martinique, one night Davis and 35 men overpowered their crewmates, and transferred anything of value from the *Mumvil Trader* to the better ship *Buck*, before sailing off.

Davis was elected captain of a crew including the former pirates Walter Kennedy, Dennis Topping, Christopher Moody and Thomas Anstis. Articles were written up for the pirates to sign, and Defoe wrote that '*He made a short speech, the sum of which was a Declaration of War against the whole World.*' They set up their base at Coxen (Coxon's) Hole, Roatán Island off Honduras. Off Hispaniola, he took a large 10-gun French vessel, and almost immediately spied a 24-gun French sloop with 60 crew. Davis knew that it would make a terrific and powerful flagship, but did not have the men or firepower to take it. Instead, he ran a black flag up on the new French prize, and sailed the *Buck* to hailing distance of the French sloop. She fired a broadside, but he shouted in response that if they continued to fight, his commander on the other approaching ship (his captured prize), would kill everyone aboard. The captured Frenchmen on the other ship had been placed upon its deck, to demonstrate Davis' 'superior' force. The subterfuge worked and the French captain surrendered. Davis favoured mercy to captured crews, but often forced men to join him. On one prize, the Welshman Richard Jones refused to sign articles, and was slashed across the leg with a sword. He was then lowered on a rope into the shark-infested waters of the Caribbean until he capitulated.

Being now hunted, Davis and his trusted lieutenants, senior pirates and former captains known as '*The House of Lords*', sailed across the Atlantic to the Cape Verde Islands. Davis sailed into the port of Sao Nicolau and was welcomed by the Portuguese garrison, pretending to be an English privateer fighting the Spanish. He stayed for 5 weeks, briefly meeting up with Edward England again, reprovisioning, and with the crew enjoying themselves so much that 5 remained on the island. The pirates were soon to sail down the African coast, looking for ships full of slaves which they could trade for gold, or ships carrying gold and goods to buy slaves, ivory and the like. He took 7 prizes, among them a two-masted brigantine off Cape Verde, upon which Davis placed 26 cannon, and renamed the *Royal James*. Failing in a raid on the Portuguese settlement of Santiago (St. Jago) in the Cape Verde Islands, he targeted the fort known as Gambia Castle, being built on the Gambia River at Gallassee. It was an English slave trade station of the Royal Africa Company, holding African slaves for transport to the New World.

Davis knew that he would lose men by attacking the fortifications, so posed as a Liverpool merchant, with a few companions all dressed in fine clothes. Davis told the governor that he had been attacked by pirates while making for Senegal to buy ivory. Barely escaping, he did not wish to return to Senegal, but wanted to purchase slaves instead. The governor showed Davis and his men around as honoured guests, with Davis making a mental note of the fort's defences, and invited the 'traders' for dinner that evening. Davis next sent some of his men to quietly take the only other vessel in the harbour, so it could not raise any alarm. 20 pirates were heavily armed and waited aboard the *Royal James* for Davis' signal, and Davis and his 'companions' arrived for dinner. Davis drew a pistol at the startled governor and told him to surrender, and then fired his second pistol through a window. His companions had positioned themselves between the governor's guards and their weapons, and pulled out their own concealed weapons and captured the guards, locking them in a room. Having captured the entire garrison, Davis then took down the flag, which was the sign for his 20 pirates to come into the castle. The men spent a day carousing at the castle, drinking all the rum and shooting the castle's cannons. Davis even convinced some of its soldiers to join them. They looted gold, ivory and around £2,000 worth of silver from the castle before setting it on fire.

The celebrating pirates spotted another ship, and battle was just avoided when they realised that it was another pirate, captained by Olivier le Vasseur, known as '*the Buzzard*'. They agreed to sail in consort and headed for Sierra Leone, where they came across the pirate Thomas Cocklyn. The 3 pirate ships then attacked on the Royal African Company's fort at Bence Island, later to be known as Freetown. After prolonged bombardment, it was taken and looted. Shortly after William Snelgrave's *Bird* was captured. Snelgrave attempted to defend his ship, and would have been killed by Cocklyn, had not the crew of the *Bird* pleaded for his life. Davis personally protected

*Christopher Moody's flag – a former pirate captain, he served as a 'lord' under Howell Davis and Bart Roberts*

fire, and as a reward, Davis gave him the Buzzard's old ship to sail home.

Soon, there was an alcohol-fuelled argument, about the next destination, between the three captains, and they parted. Davis next fought and took the Dutch *Marquis del Campo*, when a large number of his men were killed and injured. The *Marquis* was renamed *Royal Rover*, which Davis equipped with 32 cannon and 27 swivel guns. Davis then captured 3 slavers at the Bay of Annamaboe (Anomabu), Ghana. One was called the *Princess of London*, or possibly the *Princess*, out of London, and its third mate was a Pembrokeshire man like Davis, a former pirate named John Roberts. Roberts was to transmogrify into the greatest pirate of all time, 'Black Bart' Roberts, seemingly altering his surname to avoid recognition. The pirates were forced to abandon the rotting King James, which needed a new hull, and Davis sailed his Royal Rover to the Portuguese island of Principe, off the west coast of Africa. En route, he captured a Dutch ship, with the Governor of Accra and more than £15,000 on board. At Principe, the island's

Snelgrave from being tortured by Cocklyn and his crew, and took him for safety to the *Royal James*. The pirates soon discovered claret and brandy in the hold, and a massive party was held aboard the *Royal James*. In their drunken state, no-one noticed that a lantern had been dropped near the rum store, and a fire was spreading, near a store of 18 tons of gunpowder. Snelgrave organised a chain gang with buckets of water to put out the

**The slave coast of west Africa**

governor gave Davis and his crew an official welcome, believing their claim that they were Royal Navy pirate-hunters, sent to clear the region of piracy. A small French ship entered the harbour, and Davis quickly took it, saying he had been chasing it for trading with pirates. Davis had the trust of the governor, and made him a gift of 12 black slaves. He wished to lure the governor of Principe aboard *Royal Rover*, where he could be held for ransom for £40,000.

Davis invited the governor to dine on board, but a Portuguese black had escaped and swam from Davis' ship. The governor

*The death of Howell Davis in the ambush at Principe island*

pirates set off back to the ship, but were ambushed by a platoon of musketeers. 7 of the pirates were killed, including Howell Davis. According to Defoe, he was hit by 5 bullets and was killed only when his throat was cut: '...*just as he fell, he perceived he was follow'd, and drawing out his Pistols, fired them at his pursuers: Thus like a game Cock, giving a dying Blow, that he might not fall unavenged.*' Snelgrave described Davis as someone '*who, allowing for the Course of Life he had been unhappily engaged in, was a most generous humane Person*', and he took 15 ships with a value today of millions of pounds. The crew selected another captain, not from among the '*House of Lords*' of senior pirates, but the new recruit, John Roberts. On 20 June he attacked the Portuguese fort, looted it and threw its cannons into the sea. The

was informed of the ruse by the escaped prisoner the night before the invitation that they were pirates, and he set up an ambush of his own. Davis was invited to call at the governor's fort for a glass of wine, prior to escorting the governor to his ship. On 19 June 1719 Davis arrived at Government House with 9 of his men, leaving John Roberts in charge of the *Royal Rover*. The building was empty, and the town was bombarded and destroyed, and two anchored Portuguese ships were looted and burned. 'Black' Bart's career had begun (see next entry).

## 'BLACK BART' ROBERTS
## c. May 1682 – 10 February 1722

*'No, not I,' said Silver. 'Flint was*

*Milford Haven by J. Attwood (c. 1770)*

*cap'n; I was quarter-master, along of my timber leg. The same broadside I lost my leg, old Pew lost his daylights. It was a master surgeon, him that ampytated me – out of college and all – Latin by the bucket, and what not; but he was hanged like a dog, and sun-dried like the rest, at Corso Castle. That was Roberts' men, that was, and comed of changing names of their ships – Royal Fortune and so on. Now, what a ship is christened, let her stay, I says.' – Treasure Island – Robert Louis Stevenson, 1883.*

It is interesting that only 5 factual pirates were mentioned in *Treasure Island* – Captain Edward England (who sailed with Roberts in the Indian Ocean), Israel Hands, the two Welsh captains, 'Black Bart' Roberts and Howell Davis, and Roberts' surgeon. Israel Hands was hung after serving with Roberts, and Roberts' Welsh surgeon, Peter Scudamore, was said by R.L. Stevenson to have amputated Long John Silver's leg. John Roberts (later known as Black Bart Roberts) was born in the tiny hamlet of Little Newcastle (Casnewydd Bach) in Pembrokeshire. He probably went to sea aged 13, and is mentioned by Clement Downing, who served on East India Company ships in the Indian Ocean from 1717-1722, as being a pirate quartermaster and captain in 1718, arguing with the pirate captain Edward England. John Roberts had been probably pardoned under an Act of Grace, and was serving on a slave ship as 3rd mate, when captured on the Slave Coast of Guinea by Howell Davis in June 1719.(see preceding entry). Davis was shortly after killed, and senior pirates, the infamous '*House of Lords*', chose John Roberts to succeed him as their captain.

According to Defoe, the fearless Roberts accepted '*the Honour, saying, that since he had dipp'd his Hands in Muddy Water, and must be a Pyrate, it was better being a Commander than a common Man... In an honest service said he, there is thin commons* [poor food and drink], *low wages and hard labour; but in a pirate life there is plenty and satiety, pleasure and ease, liberty and power, and who would not balance creditor on this side when all the hazard that is run for it, at worst, is only a fore-look or two at choking* [dying]. *No, a merry life and a short one shall be my motto... Damnation to him who ever lived to wear a halter.*' This seems to be the origin of the phrase '*a short life and a merry one.*' The senior 'Lords' who accepted Robert included the former pirate captain Christopher Moody, whose personal pirate flag was bright red, and featured an arm with a sword flanked by a winged hourglass and a skull and crossbones. Howell Davis will have known of Roberts being a former pirate captain, through Edward England, and Valentine Ashplant, who strongly vouched for Robert as captain, also probably knew.

The teetotal John Roberts was to become known as Bartholomew Roberts, after avenging Davis' death by sacking Principe. He soon took a Dutch Guineaman and the English *Experiment*, and decided to cross the Atlantic, cruising the coast of Brazil without success for 9 weeks. The crew was becoming restless, and Roberts was close to becoming deposed when he decided to attack the Portuguese treasure fleet of 42 ships, anchored in the Bay of All Saints, off Salvador, Brazil. It was waiting for a few more ships to join and make the Atlantic crossing, and for the men. The fleet was protected by two 70-gun men-of-war, and initially his men did not wish to make the attempt, but Roberts explained his plan to infiltrate the ships at night. His two ships joined the fleet at dusk, flying Portuguese flags, and were accepted as latecomers. Quietly approaching, a longboat then took over one of the ships anchored on the fringe of the fleet, and its captain was asked to take the pirates to the most valuable prize. Roberts then drew near to the great 40-gun, 170-men flagship *Sagrada Familia*, but the captured captain shouted out a warning instead of the expected greeting.

However, the pirates quickly boarded the unsuspecting flagship, locking most of the crew below decks, and began sailing both of their prizes out of the centre of the fleet. A Portuguese man-of-war began chasing Roberts' ships and two prizes, and Roberts fired at her. She fell off, and a sailor in the crow's nest shouted that she was waiting for the other man-of-war, stationed on the other side of the fleet, to join her. By dawn the pirates had escaped to the open seas. The *Sagrada Familia* held

40,000 gold moidores (*moeda d'ouro* means gold coin), pearls, silver and jewellery. For his personal use, Roberts took a thick gold chain holding a cross of diamonds set with a huge emerald, designed for King João V of Portugal. Now admired by the House of Lords, 'Black Bart' began dressing in crimson silk from head to toe, with a scarlet ostrich-plumed hat, and the royal emerald chain when going into battle. The tall captain was known as '*le joli rouge*' by his French victims, '*the pretty man in red*', the origin of the '*Jolly Roger*', and the sight of 'the great pirate Roberts' meant that most ships surrendered rather than fight. The tall Roberts seems to have been called 'black' because of his dark skin, probably weathered at sea for over 25 years.

Gosse, in his 1932 *The History of Piracy* notes that Black Bart Roberts '*seems to attain most nearly to the popular pirate of fiction... He was remarkable, even among his remarkable companions, for several things. First of all, he only drank tea, thus being the only recorded teetotaller known to the fraternity* [of pirates]. *Also he was a strict disciplinarian and on board his ships all lights had to be out by 8pm. Any of the crew who* wished to continue drinking after that hour had to do so upon the open deck. But try as he would this ardent apostle of abstemiousness was unable to put down drinking entirely. If Roberts had lived today, he would probably have been the leading light on the council of a local vigilance society. He would allow no women aboard his ships; in fact he made a law by which any man who brought a woman on board disguised as a man was to suffer death. Nor did he permit games of cards or dice to be played for money, as he strongly disapproved of gambling. Being a strict Sabbatarian, he allowed the musicians to have a rest on the seventh say. This was as well, for the post of musician on a pirate ship was no sinecure, since every pirate had the right to demand a tune at any hour of the day or night. He used to place a guard to protect all his women prisoners and it is sadly suspicious that there was always the greatest competition amongst the worst characters in the ship to be appointed sentry over a good-looking woman prisoner. No fighting was permitted amongst his crew on board ship. All guards had to be settle don shore, the duellists standing back-to-back armed with pistol and cutlass, pirate fashion. Bartholomew dressed for action, surprisingly, was the very beau of pirates. A tall, dark man, he used to wear a rich damask waistcoat and breeches, a red feather in his cap, a gold chain round his neck with a large diamond cross dangling from it, a sword in his hand and two pairs of pistols hanging at the end of a silk sling flung over his shoulders.'

Roberts took over 400 recorded prizes in three years, across the Atlantic, the African coast and the Caribbean, and was famed as 'The Great Pyrate' – far better known at the time than Blackbeard, Captain Kidd, Edward Low and any other pirates. A teetotaller with many blacks in his crews, he did not fear attacking naval vessels belonging to Spain, France, Portugal, the Low Countries or England, whereas other pirates would flee from such powerful ships. Roberts sailed his *Royal Rover* to Devil's Island off Guiana to careen and celebrate taking the *Sagrada Familia*, and soon after took a sloop on the estuary of the Surinam River. Sighting a brigantine, Roberts chased it in his sloop, with 40 men, and left Walter Kennedy in command of the treasure-laden *Royal Rover*. Roberts was becalmed at sea for 8 days, and returning to Devil's Island, discovered that Kennedy had sailed off with the *Royal Rover* and its treasure.

Kennedy was a poor navigator, and tried to sail to Ireland but instead landed in Scotland, where 17 of his crew were arrested. In Dublin, Kennedy squandered his money, then becoming a brothel-keeper in London before being recognized, tried and finally executed on 21 July 1721. Swearing never again to take on any Irishman, Roberts renamed his sloop the *Fortune* and agreed a new pirate code, with his remaining crew signing articles.

In February 1720, Roberts took 4 ships off Barbados, and he was then joined by French pirate Montigny la Palisse in the sloop *Sea King*. The Governor of Barbados sent out 2 well-armed ships, the *Summerset* and the *Philippa*, to attack Roberts and on 26 February la Palisse and the *Sea King* quickly sailed off from the action, leaving Roberts to fight them alone. The *Fortune* sustained severe damage and only escaped by jettisoning guns to lighten the ship. Nearly all of Roberts' crew were wounded, and 20 died while sailing to Dominica to repair the *Fortune*. In March 1720, 2 armed sloops were sent by the Governor of Martinique to take Roberts, but he had just sailed north. Roberts thus swore vengeance against Barbados and

*Black Bart, 'Barti Ddu' – his commemorative stone at Casnewydd-bach (Little Newport)*

Martinique, and had another personal black flag made of himself with his emerald chain, standing upon 2 skulls, one labeled ABH (a Barbadian's Head) and the other AMH (a Martinican's Head). The heads represented the respective governors of the islands. One of his three other flags showed Roberts sharing an hourglass, with a skeleton representing Death.

Roberts began referring to himself as the '*Admiral of the Leeward Islands*', and such was his fame that he was sought out on one occasion by two ships full of would-be pirates looking for advice. He gave them guidance, weapons and ammunition. Knowing that his *Fortune* was no longer powerful enough to cruise the Caribbean, and being undermanned, Roberts sailed north to less dangerous waters, to recruit and take a better ship. The *Fortune* next raided Canso, in northern Nova Scotia, '*the oldest fishing port on mainland North America*'. It was still being fought over by the Native Americans, French and English and was a centre for fur trading, where the English were building a fort. Roberts then took a few ships on the Newfoundland banks and off Cape Breton, before sailing into Ferryland, looting around a dozen ships. On 21 June 1720, the pirates flew Robert's three flags to enter Trepassey harbour, and 22 merchant ships and 150 fishing ships were immediately deserted by their panic-stricken crews. The pirates became masters of Trepassey without any resistance being offered. Roberts was angered by the cowardice of the 22 captains who had abandoned their ships, and each morning he fired a cannon to force the captains to attend him on board the *Fortune*. They had been informed that anyone who was absent would have his ship burnt.

A fine Bristol brig was fitted out with 16 guns to replace the small sloop *Fortune*, being given the same name. The pirates left in late June, setting fire to all vessels in the harbour. In July, a flotilla of 6 French ships was taken on the Newfoundland Banks. He immediately made one, a square-rigged brig, yet another new flagship, replacing the Bristol brig. She was equipped with 26 cannons and renamed the *Good Fortune*, and his French prisoners were placed on the old *Fortune*, and left behind. Roberts wished to punish

Barbados and Martinique for their temerity in trying to capture him, with armed ships disguised as simple merchant traders. There was also little left to take on the Northern American coastline and Atlantic shipping was scarce, partially because of his depredations. With his powerful new flagship, Roberts took 4 more ships and a few boats as he returned to the West Indies, there being again joined by Montigny la Palisse's *Sea King*, which Roberts allowed to rejoin his pirate flotilla. There is a list of captured ships in this author's biography of Black Bart – by this time he had taken over 100 merchant ships – French, English, Dutch, Spanish, Danish and Portuguese – and 150 fishing vessels.

He careened his ships at Desirada, off Guadeloupe, and re-rigged his brig *Good Fortune* to make her faster and more manoeuvrable, renaming her *Royal Fortune*. On 26 September 1720 he hoisted his flags, and with his musicians playing, sailed into St. Kitts harbour, where nearly all the moored ships struck their flags. He looted 7 ships, burnt 2 for their minimal resistance and took 2 to join his fleet. The next day his sails were ripped by cannon

*Black Bart Roberts – note the gold cross of the King of Portugal*

from Basseterre Fort, as he returned to put some prisoners ashore. He sailed to St Barts to repair his ship, sell cargo and for his men to get drunk and visit the local brothels. Next, off Tortola in the Virgin Islands, the pirates took a 22-gun French brig from Martinique, which again Roberts chose as his new flagship *Royal Fortune*, adding 10 cannon. He left her French captain with an old sloop saying '*exchange is no robbery*'. 14 English and French ships were taken between 23 and 26 October, and their valuables placed in sloops acting as store ships.

The 32-gun *Royal Fortune* and 18-gun *Sea King*, firing their guns, with black flags flying, 350 pirates and musicians playing, next sailed into the harbour at St Lucia, having spotted a 42-gun Dutch 'interloper'. (An interloper was a ship, usually heavily armed, that trespassed on a trade monopoly, by conducting unauthorized trade in an area designated to a chartered company. Colonists of all nations could buy smuggled goods off them far more cheaply than from the national trade monopolies). However, its 90 men did not surrender, using booms to prevent the pirates grappling their ship, and a 4-hour fight ensued. Roberts could have blown the ship apart, but did not wish to sink her, as he desired yet another new flagship, and the smugglers were known to carry large amounts of gold. Eventually all the Dutch crew were killed, while la Palisse looted 15 other ships in the harbour. Roberts' men, thirsty for vengeance for their losses, went aboard all these boats, killing every Dutchman they could find. The Dutch ship became yet another new flagship, again renamed the *Royal Fortune*, now with 44 guns and 124 hardened pirates. The fleet also included the French brig taken off Tortola, a St Lucia sloop and the *Good Fortune*.

Yet more ships were taken and with naval vessels of all nations after him, Roberts decided to head back to Africa. Off the Cape Verde Islands he came across 2 fully laden merchant ships, escorted by 2 Portuguese men-of-war, one with 40 cannon and the other with 80 guns. He

*Black Bart Roberts before taking 11 merchantmen, showing two of his three flags (left); two of his three personal flags (right) – Bart standing on the skulls of the governors of Barbados and Martinique, and sharing the hour glass of time with Death*

ABH AMH

decided to attack, and as previously, the treacherous la Palisse sailed quickly away. However, Roberts failed to catch them and prevailing winds meant that he was pushed away from reprovisioning at the Cape Verde islands. Roberts had no chance of a landfall and calculated that the nearest point would be sailing east to Surinam, 2,100 miles away, using the trade winds. He had just one barrel of 63 gallons of water, and men began drinking their own urine or seawater, as the water blackened and ran out, to be provisioned to a swallow a day. After a terrible voyage, Roberts made Surinam, having lost some men, and reprovisioned at Tobago in December 1720.

More ships were taken, including the great Dutch brigantine *El Puerto del Principe* from Flushing. On 18 February 1721 there was a long battle with another Dutch interloper (a ship that traded smuggled goods, even to 'enemy' colonies), and all its crew were killed. Roberts now hoisted their Dutch flags and sailed up and down the Martinique shoreline, enticing boats to come out and trade with his false 'interloper'. 14 boats,

*Black Bart Roberts' crew carousing at the slave station at Old Calabar River*

filled with gold and coin for barter, were tempted out from various ports. Each was taken and its crew whipped or killed, such was Roberts' hatred of the Martinicans who had wanted him dead. 13 of the ships were burnt and the survivors put on the remaining vessel, with Roberts sending a message to the governor that he '*hoped we should always meet with such a Dutch trade as this was*'.

A Danish ship was then taken, its captain reporting that Roberts' ship had 180 white men and 48 French Creole blacks, with 42 cannon, from 4-pounders to 12-pounders, and another 7 guns. *HMS Rose* was ordered to take Roberts, but its captain, Witney, kept well away from the feared '*Great Pyrate*'. Yet more ships were taken, and in April 1721 Roberts took a French naval 32-gun man-of-war with 9 swivel guns and 140 crew off the Windward Islands. According to Walter Kennedy at his trial, the Governor of Martinique was on the ship and Roberts swung him from the yard-arm. Roberts was almost alone among pirates in attacking naval warships. On 18 April, Thomas Anstis secretly sailed off in the *Good Fortune*, which was storing most of the loot, with 100 white and 40 black crew.

Black Bart now sailed back across the Atlantic for the Cape Verde Islands, taking Dutch and English ships. The Royal Fortune was found to be unseaworthy, and was abandoned on the islands. The pirates transferred to the *Sea King*, which was renamed as yet another *Royal Fortune*. Roberts made landfall off the Guinea coast in early June, near the mouth of the Senegal River. Two French warships, one of 10 guns and one of 16 guns, gave chase, thinking Black Bart was a Dutch interloper, but surrendered when his black flags were run out. One, the *Comte de Toulouse*, was renamed the *Ranger*, while the other was named the *Little Ranger* and used as a storeship. Thomas Sutton was made captain of the *Ranger*, and James Skyrme became captain of the *Little Ranger*. *HMS Swallow* and *HMS Weymouth* had been expressly instructed to kill Roberts, and a deserter from the *Swallow*, Robert Armstrong, joined the pirates, informing Roberts of their mission. On 8 August, the pirates took two large ships off Liberia, including the frigate *Onslow*, transporting soldiers, a number of whom asking to join the pirates. The *Onslow* was converted to become the fifth *Royal Fortune*. In November and December, Roberts careened his ships and the crews caroused at Cape Lopez and Annobón Island in the Gulf of Guinea.

Black Bart took several ships in January 1722, then sailed into Whydah (Ouidah) harbour, where 10 of the 11 slavers at anchor immediately struck their colours. Each ship was ransomed, and 8 pounds of gold dust per ship was paid. The remaining vessel was set on fire at night by some angry pirates, with around 80 enslaved Africans dying on board. On 5 February 1722, *HMS Swallow*, captained by Chaloner Ogle, sighted the *Royal Fortune*, *Ranger*, and *Little Ranger* careening at Cape Lopez. She veered away to avoid a shoal, and thinking she was a fleeing merchant ship, Roberts sent James Skyrme and the *Ranger* in pursuit. Over the horizon, the *Swallow* opened her gun ports and killed 10 pirates in a broadside. Skyrme had his leg smashed off by a cannonball, but refused to leave the deck. Many of the crew did not fight, being drunk, and believing the invincible Roberts would rescue them.

On 9 February Roberts captured the *Neptune*, and his crew celebrated through the night. On 10 February, the drunken pirates thought they saw the *Ranger* returning, but it was the *Swallow*. Robert Armstrong, the deserter from the *Swallow*, recognized his old ship and ran to inform Roberts who was breakfasting in his great cabin, with Captain Hill of the captured *Neptune*. Defoe describes Bart dressing for action: '*Roberts himself made a gallant figure, at the time of the engagement, being dressed in a rich crimson damask waistcoat and breeches, a red feather in his hat, a gold chain round his neck, with a diamond cross hanging to it, a sword in his hand, and two pairs of pistols slung over his shoulders ...*' Roberts knew that if he sailed past the *Swallow*, he would be exposed to just one broadside from her, but once past the wind would allow him a good chance of escaping, while the *Swallow* would have to turn about in shallow waters. However, his inebriated helmsman steered exactly the opposite course, becalming the *Royal Fortune* and allowing the *Swallow* to deliver a second broadside. Roberts moved to sit astride a cannon, expecting death, and was killed instantly, struck by grapeshot in the throat. His crew wrapped his bejewelled body in sailcloth and weighted it with chains, throwing him overboard, as he had wished never to be taken. Only 3 pirates were killed and 272 men captured, and there occurred the greatest pirate trial of all time at Cape Corso Castle. 52 pirates were sentenced to death by hanging, and 20 men to a fairly fast death sentence in the Cape Coast mines, and 13 of 17 died in the passage to London. 72 black pirates were returned to slavery.

Of the 52 hanged men, the 18 greatest pirates such as his 'Lords' Ashplant, Sutton, Simpson, Magness and Hardy were executed first. These most important pirates were all dipped in tar and hung in chains to rot, as an example to ships outside the port. Among them was 'Israel Hinde' who had only 3 months earlier joined Roberts. The manner of his treatment must mean that he was the 'Israel Hande/Hands' who had been in Blackbeard's crew. He was thought to have died in poverty in London, after turning king's evidence against Blackbeard.

Governors of colonies from the North Americas and the Caribbean to Africa and India wrote letters giving thanks for the destruction of '*The Black Pyrate*', who had almost brought transatlantic trade to a standstill. Daniel Defoe, under the nom-de-plume Charles Johnson, had the opportunity to talk to Woodes Rogers and some of Bart's crew, and wrote in his 1724 *A General History of Pyrates* that '*the account of Roberts runs to a greater length than that of any other pyrate... because he ravaged the seas longer than the rest... having made more Noise in the World than the others*.' In the film *The Princess Bride*, the name '*Dread Pirate Roberts*' is a reference to him.

Patrick Pringle, in *Jolly Roger*, puts the Welshman's career as a pirate into true perspective: '*Most of the Guinea pirates were exceptionally daring, and one of them was possibly the most daring pirate who ever lived. His name was Bartholomew Roberts, and he bestraddles the Age of Piracy like a colossus. A Welsh poet has honoured "Black Barty", but he has never become a household name like Kidd or Blackbeard. I cannot imagine why. Not only was he immeasurably bolder, braver, and more successful – not only is his story far more exciting and dramatic – but in his lifetime he achieved a far greater fame. For nearly three years he was feared more than any other man at sea. Moreover, Johnson, on whose history most popular pirate books are based, did Roberts full justice, giving him five times as much space as Blackbeard or any other pirate ... the story of Roberts (is) one of the best documented in pirate history. This is very fortunate, for Roberts was of considerable historical as well as personal importance. He was not only the greatest of the pirates, but he was virtually the last... Captain Ogle was knighted for destroying Roberts. I think this is the only case of such an honour being granted for taking pirates, and it is a measure of the importance that was attached to the event. Bartholomew Roberts was indeed the terror of the seas, and the news of his death was acclaimed by Governors in places as far apart as New York, Port Royal, and even Bombay... It was said that the end of "the great pirate" would be the end of the great days of piracy. It was, too.*' This author's *Black Bart Roberts – The Greatest Pirate of Them All* tells his incredible story in far more detail.

## JOHN EVANS fl. 1722-1723
John Evans was a mate on ships sailing from Jamaica, and became master of a sloop sailing out of Nevis. As jobs dried up with piracy prevalent in the West Indies, he took to robbery with four other disenchanted seamen, in order to support themselves. The only alternative was being

pressed into harsh naval service or being indentured as a bond labourer on the plantations. They took a canoe out of Port Royal harbour in September 1722, and began stealing from houses near the shores of Jamaica. After a few weeks, they came across a small Bermudan sloop lying at Dun's Hole, which they took. Evans stepped aboard and announced to the crew that he was captain of their vessel, '*which was a piece of news they knew not before*'. The pirates sailed it to a small hamlet, and Evans celebrated by spending three *pistoles* on alcohol for his crew. The landlord invited captain Evans to call again, pleased with his generosity. This Evans did, in the middle of that same night, ransacking the tavern for liquor and goods to put to sea. The next day, Evans sailed for Hispaniola, in the sloop, which he now named the *Scowerer*.

They took a Spanish sloop on the very next day, the crew being able to share a sum of £150 per man. Evans then made for the Windward Isles. Off Puerto Rica they captured Captain Diamond's *Dove*, on its way from New England to Jamaica. The *Dove's* mate, with navigational knowledge, was forced to join the pirates, along with three other men. They gave the *Dove* back to Captain Diamond, and put into one of the Windward Islands for water and provisions. On January 11th, 1723, Captain Mills' 200-ton *Lucretia and Catherine* was taken, off the island of Deseada. Evans then took his men to the islet of Avis, wishing to careen the *Scowerer*. However, before they could start, they spotted a merchant sloop and gave chase, but without success, being slowed in the pursuit by the *Lucretia and Catherine*. Evans now decided to carry out a desperately needed careening at the nearby island of Ruby, but before this managed to capture a Dutch sloop. They let the *Lucretia and Catherine* go, and kept the sloop as it was a better ship. The Scowerer and the sloop now headed for the north of Jamaica, where they captured a sugar drover, then moved on to the Grand Caymans, intending to careen both ships.

Before landfall, Captain Evans and the *Scowerer's* boatswain exchanged insults, and the boatswain challenged Evans to a duel. They waited for the sloop to catch up with them before making landfall, but the boatswain refused to go ashore and fight

Evans. The angry Evans hit him around the head and shoulders with his cane, as his honour was at stake, but the boatswain drew a pistol and shot the captain in the head. The bosun then jumped overboard and tried to swim to the shore to escape the incensed crew. The *Scowerer's* longboat caught up with the bosun, and took him back aboard the ship. The majority of the pirates wished to torture him, but two of the crew were so angry that they shot him before he could be tied down. The crew could not decide upon a captain to replace the unfortunate Evans, and split £9,000 in booty amongst the 30 of them, drifting back into anonymity on the various islands in British possession.

## JOHN PHILLIPS (PHILIPS)
### d. 18th April 1724

John Phillips was probably forced from the *Inven*, the first prize captured by Thomas Anstis in the *Good Fortune*, a day after he and Thomas Jones deserted Bart Roberts. Another source says that this John Phillips had originally been captured along with Bart Roberts by Howell Davis. Anstis had not wished to sail for Africa, and Jones had been involved in a brawl with Roberts.

Phillips was needed by the pirates as a carpenter. Soon the pirates took the *Two Sisters*, under Captain Richards, and headed for Martinique. However, narrowly escaping from two French men-of-war off Montserrat, the next we hear of the *Good Fortune* in in the *Weekly Journal* of January 13th, 1722:

'Our merchants have received the following advice from St Christophers dated October 15th, 1721, that they were in daily expectation of the arrival of the new governor, with some men-of-war along with him which they very much wanted. That the Hector man-of-war, Captain Brand, having buried most of her crew could then do but little service. That several pirate ships infested the coast where one carrying thirty guns and 400 men some days before had engaged two French men-of-war. She carried a black flag at her top-mast-head. The action took place off Montserrat but she got away from them and bore away from Antigua. That five men newly come in there that did belong to the Inven, Captain Ross, from Cork in Ireland, having on board 600 barrels of beer besides other provisions which ship was taken off Martinico by a pirate sloop well mounted with 140 men. That Colonel Doyley of Montserrat *with his family was on board the said vessel and was very much cut and wounded by the pirates. That 21 of these brutes had forced a woman passenger one after another and afterwards broke her back and threw her into the sea.*' Doyley had been attacked for trying to defend the woman – the story shows how remarkable the discipline of Captain Bart Roberts was, regarding the safety of women.

Anstis and Jones next captured Captain Marston's ship carrying alcohol and provisions, and five men joined the crew, before taking Captain Smith's *Hamilton* in late June 1722. At Mohair Key, the crew laid up for a few weeks, to drink their way through the liquor and careen the *Good Fortune*. They returned the looted and stripped *Hamilton* to its captain, and headed for the Gulf of Campeachy, taking two Spanish ships on the way, with meagre returns. One was driven ashore at Campeachy and one was burned. Strangely, the next ship they encountered was again Captain Smith's *Hamilton*. It had been captured by a Spanish privateers, and was being taken into Cuba when the Spaniard ran aground. Jones asked Smith if he had been looking for his empty bottles, before he was put into an open boat with his remaining crew, and the *Hamilton* was burnt. On October 21st, the rich *Don Pedro* was looted off Hispaniola, the first decent prize since Anstis and Jones had deserted Roberts. £3000 in goods was taken, and its surgeon forced to join, after a short battle when two of its crew were killed.

A few days later, the *Morning Star* was captured, 32 guns were transferred to her, and the one-handed John Finn was elected captain. The *Morning Star* and *Good Fortune* took Captain Lubbock's *Portland* in December, then two more small prizes before taking Captain Ellwood's *Nightingale*, at anchor of Tortuga. This was April 1722, and while the pirates careened, the former members of Roberts' crew must have mused upon the poor 'luck' of Anstis as a leader. Roberts concentrated on specific areas to hunt, whereas Anstis seemed to have no strategy but to rely on ships passing at sea. Some wanted to steal the *Good Fortune*, and Anstis was replaced in an election as its captain by Bridstock Weaver. The unhappy pirates allowed Ellwood to sail off in the *Nightingale* upon condition he took the following petition for pardon to Governor Lawes of Jamaica and return with an answer:

*To His Most Gracious majesty, by the Grace of God, of Great Britain, France, and Ireland, Defender of the Faith*

*The Humble PETITION of the Company, now belonging to the Ship Morning Star and Brigantine Good Fortune, lying under the ignominious Name and Denomination of Pyrates, Humbly sheweth: That we your Majesty's most loyal Subjects have, at sundry Times, been taken by Bartholomew Roberts, the then Captain of the aforesaid Vessels and Company, together with another Ship, in which we left him, and have been forced by him and his wicked Accomplices, to enter into, and serve, in the said Company; as Pyrates, much contrary to our Wills and Inclinations: and we, your loyal Subjects utterly abhorring and detesting that impious Way of Living, did, with a unanimous Consent, and contrary to the Knowledge of the said Roberts or his Accomplices, on, or about, the 18th Day of April, 1721, leave, and ran away with, the aforesaid Ship Morning Star and Brigantine Good Fortune with no other Intent and Meaning than the Hopes of obtaining your Majesty's most gracious Pardon. And that we, your Majesty's most loyal subjects, may with more Safety return to our native Country and serve the Nation, unto which we belong, in our respective Capacities, without Fear of being prosecuted by the Injured, whose Estates have suffered by the said Roberts and his Accomplices, during our forcible Detainment, by the said Company. We most humbly implore your Majesty's most royal Assent, to this our humble Petition. And your Petitioners shall ever pray etc.*

The forced carpenter, John Phillips, and Thomas Jones sailed with Ellwood with the petition, as they were both confident of a reprieve. Jones said he was pressed by Roberts and escaped from him, and Phillips had been forced as an 'artist'. Governor Lawes sent the petition to London, having received in on July 6th. By the time the various authorities in London had decided to pardon the pirates, the August deadline given by the pirates had passed, and they returned to piracy. Phillips managed to return to England on the *Nightingale*. Learning that some of his co-pirates under Anstis had been taken to gaol in Bristol, he panicked and quickly decided to try to sail to Newfoundland, leaving Topsham harbour. Having failed to gain a pardon, Phillips had remained 'under cover' in Bristol, as he felt that his story of being 'forced' would not be believed. (Thomas Jones, the old comrade of Howell Davis, who sailed under Bart Roberts, and had deserted with Anstis, was one of those arrested – he was sent to the Marshalsea Prison in London, and later executed).

Upon landing at Peter Harbour Phillips deserted his ship, and became a splitter in a cod-fishery. The work was terribly hard, in freezing conditions, but was safer and easier than being a merchant seaman in those days. Roberts had easily recruited such men in his raids on neighbouring Trepassy, and Phillips soon grew tired of an honest life. He had tasted the fruits of the easy life of piracy, and it beckoned him stongly. On August 29th, 1723, with William White he stole a small schooner belonging to a William Minors (or Minott), off Saint Pierre Island. White was one of Minors' crewmen. Sixteen disaffected men had plotted the capture, but only four turned up, so they sailed away with three others Phillips being chosen as captain. White had no position, but John Nutt was sailing-master, James Sparks the gunner, and Thomas Fern the carpenter. Articles were drawn up, and in the absence of a *Bible*, they swore them over a hatchet. Defoe enumerates Phillips' articles on board the *Revenge*:

1. *Every Man shall obey civil Command; the Captain shall have one full Share and a half in all Prizes; the Master, carpenter, Boatswain and Gunner shall have one Share and a quarter*

2. *If any Man shall offer to run away, or keep any Secret from the Company, he shall be marooned, with one Bottle of Powder, one Bottle of Water, one small Arm and shot.*

3. *If any Man steal any Thing in the Company, or game to the Value of a Piece of Eight, he shall be marooned or shot.*

4. *If at any Time we should meet another Marooner (that is, Pyrate) that Man shall sign his Articles without the Consent of our Company, shall suffer such Punishment and the Captain and Company shall think fit.*

5. *That man that shall strike another whilst these Articles are in force, shall receive Moses' Law (that is, 40 Stripes lacking one) on the bare Back.*

6. *That man that shall snap his Arms, or smoke Tobacco in the Hold, without a Cap*

*to his Pipe, or carry a Candle lighted without a Lanthorn, shall suffer the same Punishment as the former Article.*

7. *That Man that shall not keep his Arms clean, fit for an Engagement, or neglect his Business, shall be cut off from his Share, and suffer such other Punishment as the Captain and the Company think fit.*

8. *If any Man shall lose a Joint in Time of an Engagement, he shall have 400 Pieces of Eight, if a Limb, 800.*

9. *If at any Time we meet with a prudent Woman, that Man offers to meddle with her, without her Consent, shall suffer present Death.*

By taking several small fishing boats, Phillips added to his crew. A former pirate named Burrill became boatswain. One of his prisoners from a merchantman was the ex-pirate John Rose Archer, who had served under the infamous Blackbeard, Edward Thache, in 1718. Archer was quickly made quartermaster. Phillips called his ship the *Revenge*, and in October 1723 captured another Welshman, William Phillips. In that month, the brig *Mary*, another brig, a Portuguese brig and the sloop *Content* were taken, with reasonable takings off each prize. From the *Content*, its first mate John Master, William Phillips, William Taylor and James Wood were 'forced'. The crew holed up and careened in a small bay on Barbados for several weeks, but ran desperately short of provisions, so returned to sea.

Phillips spotted a large 12-gun Martinican ship with 35 crew, and was forced to attack it for much-needed supplies. It tried to outsail the *Revenge*, which took almost a day to overhaul her, and after bitter fighting it was taken. Four of the survivors, one a surgeon, were impressed as pirates, and the ship reprovisioned. Two more ships were taken, then the *Revenge* was careened again, in Tobago. Anstis had careened there with Phillips, and Phillips wanted more men for his crew. Some pirates had hidden there in the recent past, members of the crews of Anstis and Finn when they were attacked. However, he only found one marooned black, Pedro, who said that the other men had been taken off by a man-of-war. The *Revenge* now beat a hasty retreat when a man-of-war was spotted by Burrill, taking on water nearby, and the four French prisoners were left behind.

Several more ships were taken, with more violence than was necessary. They included a sloop from New York, a Virginia ship under Captain Haffam, three Jamaican sloops, a snow and a Portuguese ship bound for Brazil. In February 1724, John Phillips put William Phillips and four others on board Captain Laws' captured snow, with Thomas Fern as captain, ordering them to sail in consort with the *Revenge*. One night, the consort attempted to elude the *Revenge*, but was chased for several hours and taken in a savage battle when James Wood was killed. William Phillips had to have his left leg amputated. There was no ship's surgeon, so John Rose Archer, with some experience of these matters, sawed Phillips' leg off. He then used a red-hot axe to cauterise the stump. However, he burned too much of Phillips' body away from the wound area, leaving terrible injuries. William Taylor had also been injured in the leg. Heading north from Tobago, a Portuguese ship and three sloops were taken, and Fern again tried to escape in one of the sloops. He was shot by Captain Phillips, in accordance with the ship's articles, and another seaman a few days later for the same offence. Over 30 French, English, American and Portuguese ships were taken in nine months in the West Indies and along the Atlantic Coast.

On February 7th, 1724, Captain Huffan's ship was taken off North Carolina. The navigator Harry Gyles was forced, as was Charles Ivemay, but John Masters was allowed to leave, as he had a wife and children who would starve without his income. On March 25th, another two ships were taken, one under another John Phillips, and one under Captain Robert Mortimer. On March 27th, Mortimer struck Phillips with a hand-spike in the shoulder, while trying to lead a mutiny. But his men stood by and Phillips slashed him with his sword three times, then Nutt and Archer hacked at his prostrate body before Burrill kicked it and ordered Mortimer's crew to throw his body overboard. John Salter's sloop off the Isle of Sabloes was next taken on April 4th, and kept as a prize. Captain Caldwell's schooner was also captured and Phillips was about to scuttle it when he discovered that it was owned by the Mr Minors who had 'supplied' him with the *Revenge*, so he let it go. A ship under Captain Dependance Ellery was taken, but it had tried to outrun the pirates, so they forced the unfortunate master to dance until he dropped with exhaustion.

Ten vessels were shortly taken, with the following masters, Joshua Elwell, Samuel Elwell, Mr Combs, Mr Lansley, James Babston, Edward Freeman, Mr Start, Obadiah Beal, Erick Erickson and Benjamin Wheeler. In early April 1724, when Phillips took two ships travelling from Virginia to New York. From the *Dolphin*, Edward Cheeseman and John Filmore, (the great-grandfather of President Millard Fillmore) were forced to become pirates. Phillips replaced his ship with the *Dolphin*, which was a better sailer, a sloop out of Cape Ann.

Phillips sailed back up to Newfoundland, intending to take on more crew from the disaffected cod-splitting fraternity, and off Nova Scotia took Andrew Harradine's brand-new sloop on April 17th. Harradine quickly discovered that over half the crew were forced men, and were anxious to be rid of Phillips. A day later, Harradine, Fillmore, Cheesman and some other forced men attacked the pirates with axes and hammers. The desperate Phillips tripped over, and was killed by Captain Harridan's hatchet. Phillips' head was cut off, pickled and tied to the mast-head. Archer and the few pirates were overpowered. The gunner James Sparks and John Nutt were thrown overboard by Edward Cheeseman in the mutiny.

The remainder of John Phillips' crew were chained up, and Harridan took the ship to land in Boston on May 3rd. Cheeseman and Fillmore were tried in Boston on May 12th and acquitted, while Archer and White were found guilty. Phillips and Burrill's heads, pickled in Newfoundland, were exhibits at the trial. Some of Phillips' personal treasures were awarded by the court to Fillmore, including silver knee-buckles, shoe buckles, a tobacco box, a silver-hilted sword and two gold rings. Archer, William Phillips and William White were hung on Bird Island in Boston Harbour on June 2nd. They were ministered to in their last days by a fierce Boston theologian, of whom John Jameson remarked in 1923 that '*Cotton Mather ministered to them in their last days, adding, one would think a new horror to death*'. The amputee William Phillips was somehow reprieved after conviction, as was William Taylor. The negro Pedro was acquitted, as was another impressed negro known as Pierro, and three impressed Frenchmen, John Baptis, Peter Tafferey and Isaac Lassen.

## JAMES WILLIAMS d. 1725

Williams was on the *George* galley sailing out of Amsterdam in 1724. From Santa Cruz on the Barbary Coast, they took on a cargo of beeswax to Genoa. However, with the Scots second mate John Gow (alias Smith or Goffe) Williams conspired among the crew to mutiny. After they left Genoa on November 3rd, 1724. Captain Ferneau of Guernsey, the chief mate and the surgeon were killed at night.

Gow was elected Captain and Williams' chief mate, as the men decided to '*go on the account.*' The *George* was renamed the *Revenge*, armed with 18 guns, and an English sloop under Captain Thomas Wise was taken off the Spanish coast, filled with fish from the Newfoundland banks. Another prize, a Glasgow ship with a cargo of herrings and salmon was next taken. In Madeira, Gow presented the Governor with a box of Scotch herrings. A large French ship was next spotted, but Gow refused to chase and attack it. Williams accused Gow of cowardice, and fired his pistol into Gow's face in the ensuing argument, but it failed to go off. Two of Gow's pirates then shot Williams, severely wounding him in the arm and stomach. The next day, Captain Gow released some prisoners in an old sloop, manacling Williams and throwing him into the hold. The released captives were told to give Williams up as a pirate to the first English man-of-war they encountered. At Lisbon he was put on board *HMS Argyle* and taken to London.

Gow now sailed to the Orkneys to traffic in his stolen goods, but 11 men deserted. One bought a horse for three pieces-of-eight and rode to Kirkwall to surrender, and the other ten were taken prisoner near Edinburgh. After plundering the countryside, Gow ran the *Revenge* on rocks off the Isle of Eda, and his crew were captured. Gow and his crew were taken in chains to the Marshalsea prison, where they found Williams already incarcerated. Two attempts were made to hang Gow. On the same day, June 11th 1725, Williams was hanged at Newgate, and his body hung in chains at Blackwall Dock alongside that of his enemy Captain Gow.

**CAPTAIN ROBERT JENKINS fl. 1731-38**

The War of Jenkin's Ear (which merged into the War of the Austrian Succession, when France joined Spanish forces in 1744) was the result, amongst other things, of a minor confrontation between Spanish *Guarda Costas* and the Welsh Captain and crew of the Glasgow brig '*Rebecca*' in 1731. Captain Robert Jenkins claimed that, whilst in the Caribbean, his ship had been boarded by the Guarda Costa and his crew maltreated, and that the Spaniards had then cut off one of his ears. Additionally, he claimed he was tortured and threatened with death. Jenkins had relieved a Spanish salvage party of treasure that they were bringing up from a wrecked Spanish galleon. The *guarda costa* stopped British vessels, against the Treaty of Utrecht, because their trade laws prohibited British commerce with Spanish colonies. Although the incident occurred in 1731, it was only bought before Parliament in 1738, at a time when it was investigating Spanish depredations in the Caribbean. The situation in the Caribbean had been thought serious enough that four ships and two sloops had previously been despatched to the Caribbean to protect British commerce there. In 1738 Parliament was trying to ascertain the number of ships that had been taken by the Spanish.

Whether Jenkin's claims were true was by no means certain, but it was true that he had had part of his ear cut off, and his story was received with universal indignation. He told Parliament that the Spanish captain had given him back his ear, with the message that he would do exactly the same to the English King if he had the chance. Great Britain, aroused by the tales of mistreatment of her merchant seamen (notably the display by Robert Jenkins of his shrivelled ear to Parliament) and other hostile acts (provoked by British abuses of the Asiento and activities of her logwooders of the Honduran coast as well as by the unsettled Florida Border), declared war on Spain (19 Oct. 1739). Robert Walpole's declaration of war '*was received by all ranks and distinctions of men with a degree of enthusiasm and joy, which announced the general frenzy of the nation.*' There were no major actions fought during this war, although the declaration of war led to the despatch of Admiral Anson's squadron to attack the coast of

South America, and Admiral Edward Vernon's fleet attacked Spanish territory in the Caribbean.

Basically, the war was one of commercial rivalry between England and Spain. By the Treaty of Utrecht (1713), which ended Queen Anne's war, Britain was allowed to participate in slave traffic with the Spanish colonies. A special Spanish fleet, however, interfered with this activity and the Spanish also objected to the English logwooders operating on the coast of Honduras. The other cause of the war was the continued dispute over the boundary of Spanish Florida in relation to Georgia. As soon as war was declared, Gov. James Edward Oglethorpe called on the citizens of Georgia and South Carolina to join in an invasion of Florida. The Spanish retaliated by attempting to invade those colonies by sea.

The War of Jenkins' Ear (1739-1742) continued with an invasion of Florida led by Oglethope. He was protected on the west from the French by friendly Creek, Cherokee and Chickasaw Indians. He captured forts San Francisco de Pupo and Picolata on the San Juan River. From May to July he besieged St. Augustine, but broke off the attack when his rear guard was threatened by the Spanish. In the Battle of Bloody Marsh on St. Simon's Island, one of the Sea Islands off the south-east coast of Georgia, the Spanish attacked Fort Frederica, which had been constructed by Oglethorpe in 1736 to protect the colony. The Spanish were repulsed in a bloody battle that was a decisive engagement of The War of Jenkins' Ear.

## CHRISTOPHER BASSETT d. 1760

This Bonvilston man was related to the Bassetts of Old *Beaupré* castle, and around 1760 was given letters of marque to go privateering. In his brief career, he collected as much as £10,000 for one of his 'prizes'. He built a folly on The Gaer, at Bonvilston, with part of the proceeds.

## THOMAS KNIGHT fl. 1783

A 1734 letter from local customs officers to the London authorities reads: '*At Aberthaw and Barry when any boat goes out to em from thence, the Owners of em have always a Spye on the officer; and when they find him on one side of the River of Aberthaw, they'll land what they have of the other; and by reason*

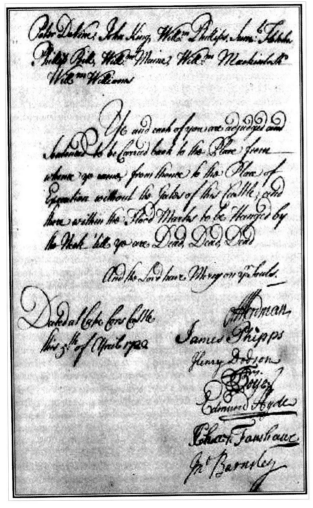

there's no Boat in the Service, nor any boat on those acco'ts to be had for love or money, and the Officer obliged to go to a bridge about two Miles round, they have time enough to secure the goods before he can get there. Nay, there is instances that they have run'd goods in the day time before the officers face in this Manner. At Barry tis the same case; if they find the officer on the Iseland they'll land the other side of the harbour. If the other Side of the harbour, they'll land on the Iseland, and the officers can't get over till the Tide is out, wich may be five or six hours; and there is so much Cover on the Iseland, and such conveniencys for hiding of goods the other side, that an Officer has but a poor Chance to meet with em after they are landed.'

Until 1743, Customs Officers were unarmed, and always under-resourced to cope

1722 Warrant for the hanging of 19 of Roberts' crew until they are 'Dead, Dead, Dead'

with desperate smugglers, who knew that capture was execution. As a result, many officials took the easy option and supplemented their meagre wages by accepting bribes. After 1743, however, we see continuous requests for decent boats to make reasonable patrols in coastal waters. On February 3, 1764, two Customs men were drowned when their boat returned from inspecting Flat and Steep Holm islands. There was also a case in 1773 when the local customs boat was in too poor a condition to police the activities on Flat Holm, and the King's officers refused to go out in rough seas.

In 1783, Thomas Knight moved from Lundy to make Barry Island his base for smuggling. He had an armed brig, with 40 men and 24 cannon. The local Customs officer, or 'searcher' was Thomas Hopkins of Sully, who was absolutely powerless to control Knight's activities, but with reinforcements managed to push him back to Lundy around 1787. He was driven from Barry Island by Customs Officers who fought a pitched battle, and recovered a huge cache of brandy and port. Knight had also used the Old Swan Inn at Llantwit Major (Llanilltud Fawr) as a headquarters

for smuggling. However, a Captain Arthur, even more of a rogue than Knight, then occupied Barry Island, and two expeditions were needed in 1788 to force him off the Island. The last use of the island as a smugglers' retreat seems to have been in 1791 when a crew operated the *John of Combe* from there.

## O'NEILL

Until the 1850's, May 3rd saw the great event of Llanilltud Festival. It commemorated the date that the great pirate O'Neill attacked the town. The townspeople planned carefully to deal with his next attack, and hid in the gorse on both sides of the Col-huw valley as he approached the town. They then poured down the hills cutting off his retreat and in the melée several villagers, pirates and O'Neill himself were killed. His body was buried on the hillside there on the 3rd of May, and it became the town's holiday, *Annwyl Day* for centuries. Each anniversary attackers and defenders were selected from the neighbouring coastal communities of Boverton, Llanilltud Fawr (Llantwit Major) and St Donats. Tents were placed in Colhuw valley and the 'pirates' would approach up the valley, to be beaten and captured by the defenders. The young men of Boverton and St Donats on horseback would lead the captured men and a great effigy of O'Neill, which was then burnt. The 'pirates', with blackened faces and eye-patches, would be led as prisoners through the town to the Court of Justice. There were sporting contests, dancing and singing, but the custom died out around 1850, the same time as the remarkable St Illtud's Feast Day celebrations – both events should be revived.

## WILLIAM WILLIAMS c. 1727-1791 – the Marooned Privateer, Artist, Polymath and 'Author of the First American Novel', the 'Forgotten Genius'

Around 1786, an impoverished artist was befriended by the literary critic Reverend Thomas Eagles, who found him lodgings in the Merchant Venturers' Almshouses in Bristol. The painter's bedroom can even today be visited. The old man had been a successful painter in colonial America, and was known to Eagles as '*Lewellin Penrose*'. Penrose became very friendly with Eagles' family, and in 1791 Eagles was surprised to be Penrose's sole beneficiary in his deathbed will. His family only now discovered that Lewellin Penrose was actually William Williams. Williams had been forced to leave New York because the War of Independence left him with no livelihood of teaching music and painting (many of his paintings are in art galleries).

Williams left the Reverend Eagles a

*Old Beaupré castle*

manuscript written in the Americas, detailing his joining a Bristol privateer and being captured by the Spanish, imprisoned in Havana, and finally joining a privateer again before being marooned off the Miskito Coast of Nicaragua. Williams left all his possessions to Thomas Eagles, including this factional *The Journal of Penrose, Seaman*. In 1805, fourteen years after Williams' death, the great American artist Benjamin West RA was visiting Thomas Eagles' London town house. Luckily, as he waited for Eagles, West happened to notice William's manuscript lying upon a table. West then borrowed the manuscript, telling Thomas Eagles' son John that he had known Williams, aka 'Penrose', both in America and London. Williams had initially inspired, and indeed then taught West to paint. West honestly believed the *Journal* to be a true account of Williams' life as a privateer, and that Williams had been marooned among the Indians. The places mentioned in the text – the islands, reefs, caves and coastline – have all been identified in Nicaragua. The Rev. Eagles' son John himself had heard 'Penrose' recounting his years on the Nicaraguan coastline.

Written perhaps around 1775 by the unknown privateer and polymath, William Williams, the book is an account of living among the Rama Indians of the Miskito Coast. It is a superb evocation of an almost idyllic existence, and in effect an astonishing natural history of the area – its

*The Old Swan, Llanilltud Fawr (Llantwit Major)*

jungle, shoreline, sea and islands. There are described at least 36 different species of birds, 48 different trees, shrubs, fruit and vegetables, 36 fish, 11 crabs and shells, 14 mammals, 24 reptiles, 20 insects, 7 turtles and tortoises, plus crustaceans and invertebrates totalling around 200 known animals and plants. All these fish, plants and animals mentioned by Penrose are native to the Atlantic seaboard and rainforest of Nicaragua. The indigenous Rama tribe which supported him is now facing extinction, and their customs are described in some detail.

Williams' *The Journal of Penrose, Seaman* contains entries covering 27 years spent on the rainforest shoreline, and reads almost as if it is written in the 21st century, with strong feelings against slavery and religious bigotry running as themes throughout the book. The author's attitudes towards racial and female equality, in a time of universal slavery, are simply astonishing, as is his positing of a 'savage' native civilization being far more humane and rational, than many aspects of the Christian church. The Reverend Thomas Eagles and his son John altered the original manuscript to produce a book, not published until 1815, 24 years after Williams' death. It was the literary sensation of its day. Proof-read by Sir Walter Scott, this was a heavily expurgated edition, but was still highly lauded by the Poet Laureate Robert Southey, who believed it to be true.

The *Journal* was ecstatically reviewed by Lord George Byron. '*I have never read so much of a book in one sitting in my life. He (Penrose) kept me up half the night, and made me dream of him the other half... it has all the air of truth, and is most interesting and entertaining in every point of view.*' It is also thought that Penrose's Journal influenced Lord Grey to later enact the first anti-slavery laws, when he became Prime Minister. It is also the first novel written in America by around 15 years, and should be on all academic syllabi, also being suitable for a film script. It was widely praised as being vastly superior to *Robinson Crusoe* (published in 1719), as Daniel Defoe had never experienced the vicissitudes of William Williams.

The book is a plea for racial and religious tolerance, but much more than that, a marvellous adventure story based upon its author running away from

# the Journal of Penrose; Seaman.

If ever the following lines should reach my dear country, the Reader is not to expect to meet with any persuasive Arguments to enforce belief, or language to adorn the story, as the Author never received more learning than what a common country school affords. In the first place, I shall give the reader a faithful Narrative of every occurence within my memory, from the day of my birth, unto the time I first left my native shore, to cross the Atlantic.

Lewellin Penrose is my name. I was born near Caerphilly in Glamorgan shire, in the month of May, anno dom 1725. My father who was a Sailor, was castaway in a Ship belonging to the city of Bristol, called the Union Frigate commanded by a certain Capt. Williams who was his own countryman, in the great January Storm at the Texel in Holland where every soul perished of a fleet consisting of near 60 Sail of Vessels, only one Dutch Dogger which lay without, riding it safe the whole time.

My Mother being left a Widow, with two children (vizt) myself and a Sister five years younger, after a time, married a School-master, and removed with him into Worcestershire, thence into Monmouth shire and after that into Wales. This man, I may justly remark, at least in my own opinion, proved the innocent or rather ultimate cause of many hardships I have since his days, undergone, as I learnt a few years after his death.

58

the Round Robbin Exactly transcribed from the Original Manuscript, as faithfully made out as the Badness of the Characters and blindness of ye Ink would admit. NB. those names, to which crops are added, were such as could not writ[e]

as I judge, and I take notice, there are Negros names among the rest, such as Sambo, Cudjoe and perhaps some others of them, were of the mixed breed, as the principal character necessary to become one of such a Banditty, was that of being an approved reprobate. If he could one[ly] recommend himself, capable of Robbing Father Brother or Relation. Force a Rape on Maid, Wife or Widow. Swear Black, was White or the contrary, or even Stow a poor unfortunate Man in Davy Jones's locker, he was then the man fit to be Sworn in, as what they Styled a good Fellow.

*First page of William Williams' manuscript factional novel*

*A 'round robin' signed where buried treasure was found by Lewellin Penrose*

Caerphilly, Wales to sea in 1744, and being marooned in the coastal rainforests of Central America until his death in 1775. Of the author himself, in 1946 the art critic James Thomas Flexner wrote of: '*The amazing William Williams: Painter, Author, Teacher, Musician, Stage Designer, Castaway... The activities of this forgotten genius spread across almost every branch of American culture... he will stand out as a significant figure in the development of American culture.*' This forgotten author was a polymath – a privateer, poet, music-teacher, naturalist, writer and painter who inspired and taught Colonial America's greatest artist Benjamin West, built America's first permanent theatre and wrote America's first novel.

Of special importance in the text is the discovery of mammoth bones in the rainforest by Penrose (aka Williams), along with basalt pillars with hieroglyphics. These have only been discovered in Nicaragua in the last 40 years. The book itself is superbly written faction, and contains the '*first story of buried treasure*', which inspired Edgar Allan Poe to write *The Gold Bug* and saved him from bankruptcy. It is also the first known account of a message in a bottle. *The Journal of Penrose, Seaman* was strongly anti-slavery at a time when Presidents Washington, Jefferson and Adams had slaves, and the reason that it is still barely known is a mystery.

America's first novel, written by a privateer polymath, is an astounding and inspirational piece of writing, an exciting adventure story worthy of international renown. This author has studied rewritten the original manuscript (in the holdings of the Lilly Library, Indiana University, Bloomington), with notes and a biography of Williams, as *The First American Novel: The Journal of Penrose, Seaman by William Williams, & the Book, the Author and the Letters in the Lilly Library* (2007), and a modernized version as *The Journal of Penrose, Seaman – the New Robinson Crusoe* (2014).

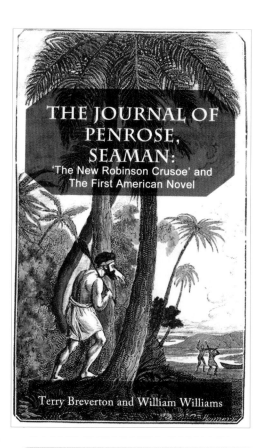

THE JOURNAL OF
PENROSE,
SEAMAN:
'The New Robinson Crusoe' and
The First American Novel

Terry Breverton and William Williams

The first American novel, written by the
privateer William Williams

## THE TRUE CONFESSIONS OF
# WILLIAM OWEN
### SMUGGLER,
### PRIVATEER
### AND MURDERER

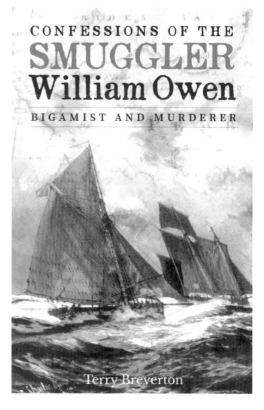

The writing of this book became a detective story. It began as a straightforward modernised transcription of a condemned murderer's confession, but contradictions had to be explored. Along the way, we become acquainted with the rogue John Lilly, Owen's adversary then accomplice, whom Owen killed to escape a hue and cry on Lilly's horse. We discover where he shot Lilly, on a field then renamed Cae Lilly, and that some of his remarkable claims were indeed true. We find out that he committed bigamy, and examine the trial where he was oddly acquitted of murdering customs officers. A strange man, who thought nothing of killing unarmed men in cold blood, admitted to many affairs, visiting brothels and fathering illegitimate children, yet despised drunkenness, the book examines the truth and lies of his remarkable life.

## www.carreg-gwalch.cymru

## COMPACT CYMRU
– MORE TITLES;

**FULL OF COLOUR IMAGES
AND CONCISE WRITING**

**www.carreg-gwalch.cymru**

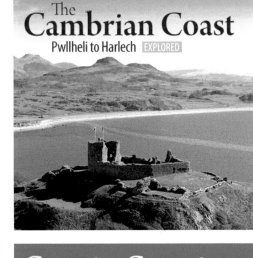

The
Cambrian Coast
Pwllheli to Harlech EXPLORED

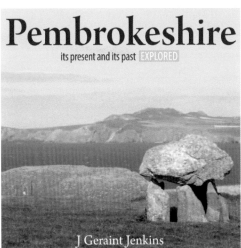

Pembrokeshire
its present and its past EXPLORED

J Geraint Jenkins

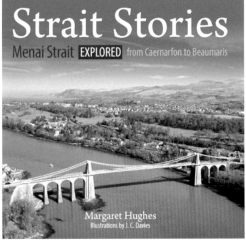

Strait Stories
Menai Strait EXPLORED from Caernarfon to Beaumaris

Margaret Hughes
Illustrations by J. C. Davies

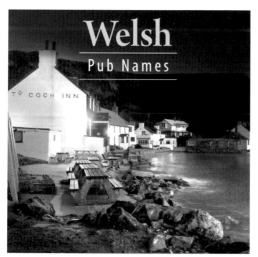

# Welsh
## Pub Names

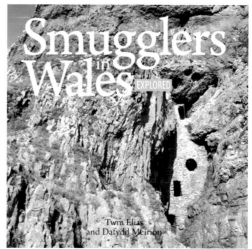

# Smugglers
# in Wales EXPLORED

Twm Elias
and Dafydd Meirion

# Iconic
# Cycling
## Trails in Wales

Phil Horsley

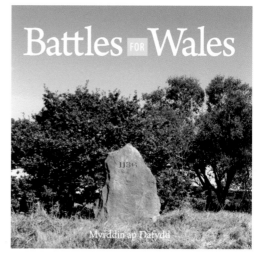

# Battles FOR Wales

Myrddin ap Dafydd

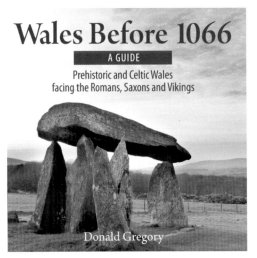

# Wales Before 1066
## A GUIDE
Prehistoric and Celtic Wales
facing the Romans, Saxons and Vikings

Donald Gregory

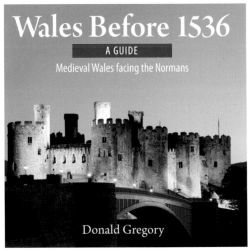

# Wales Before 1536
## A GUIDE
Medieval Wales facing the Normans

Donald Gregory

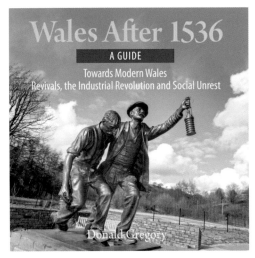

# Wales After 1536
## A GUIDE
Towards Modern Wales
Revivals, the Industrial Revolution and Social Unrest

Donald Gregory

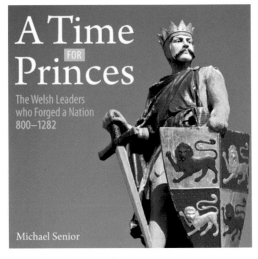

# A Time FOR Princes
The Welsh Leaders
who Forged a Nation
800–1282

Michael Senior

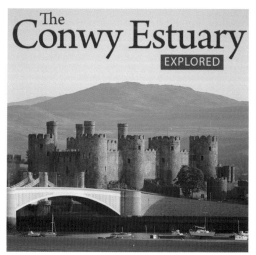

# The
# Conwy Estuary
EXPLORED

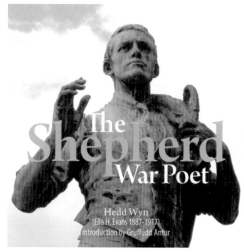

# The
# Shepherd
## War Poet

Hedd Wyn
(Ellis H. Evans 1887-1917)
introduction by Gruffudd Antur

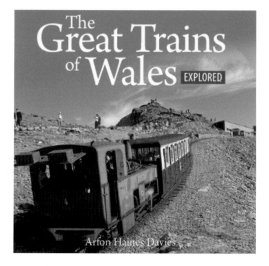

# The
# Great Trains
## of Wales EXPLORED

Arfon Haines Davies

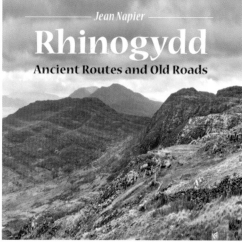

*Jean Napier*

# Rhinogydd
## Ancient Routes and Old Roads

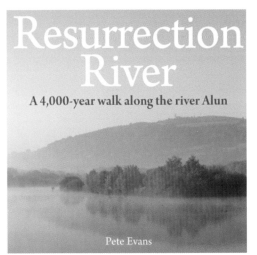

# Resurrection River
## A 4,000-year walk along the river Alun

Pete Evans

# Snowdon
## Villages and its
### EXPLORED

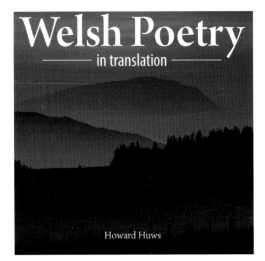

# Welsh Poetry
## in translation

Howard Huws

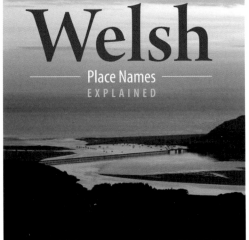

# Welsh
## Place Names
### EXPLAINED